What can I do with...

No Degree?

trotman

What can I do with...

No Degree?

Second Edition

Margaret McAlpine

What can I do with...no degree?
Second edition

This second edition published in 2004 by Trotman and Company Ltd
2 The Green, Richmond, Surrey TW9 IPL

© Trotman and Company Limited 2004

Editorial and Publishing Team
Author Margaret McAlpine
Editorial Mina Patria, Editorial Director; Rachel Lockhart,
Commissioning Editor; Anya Wilson, Editor.
Production Ken Ruskin, Head of Pre-press and Production
Sales and Marketing Deborah Jones, Head of Sales and Marketing
Managing Director Toby Trotman

British Library Cataloguing in Publication Data
A catalogue record for this book is available from the British Library

ISBN 0 85660 951 X

Typeset by Mac Style Ltd, Scarborough, N. Yorkshire

Printed and bound in Great Britain by Creative Print & Design Group
(Wales) Ltd

Contents

About the author

Margaret McAlpine taught for a number of years in schools and colleges in the Midlands and East Anglia before becoming a journalist. Today she writes for a number of publications and has a particular interest in writing careers material for young people. She has three grown-up children and lives with her husband in Suffolk.

Acknowledgements

My thanks to the staff at the Bury St Edmunds Connexions office for their good-humoured support, to Pam for her eagle eye and good ideas and to Rod for his help in so many ways.

Introduction

You don't need a degree to get on in life.

There are lots of interesting jobs with good prospects open to people who have not been to university, and many intelligent young people choose to go into work at either 16 or 18. There are many reasons for this. Some need or want to start earning money as soon as possible. Others haven't particularly enjoyed school and are ready for a change. For others a Saturday job or a hobby has fired an interest in a particular type of work. Whatever the reason thousands of young people every year make a positive decision to take a job, one which offers training and good prospects for the future.

Going to university is expensive. The National Union of Students calculates that the average cost of a degree is almost £20,000. At present universities charge students tuition fees of £1125 a year. But the introduction of top-up fees would allow them to charge an average of around £5000 a year and more for some courses.

Choosing what to do

Some jobs such as medicine, dentistry and physiotherapy need a degree. There are other jobs for which it is a strong advantage to have a degree. For example, non-graduates do become solicitors, but the training takes a long time and a great many trainees give up on the way.

The first step towards deciding what to do after leaving school, and even when to leave school, is to consider the sort of job you want – working in an office, a laboratory, out of doors, with children, with animals, with machinery? Do you want a chance to travel, or do you want to work close to home?

A good place to carry out this sort of investigation is a Connexions office, where there are interactive computer programs designed to pinpoint your particular interests and to identify job possibilities with trained careers staff on hand to give advice.

Learning or doing

Some people are doers not learners. They flourish once they leave the classroom behind and can concentrate on developing practical skills. Such people often surprise themselves and others once they find themselves in a working situation that suits them.

Whether you enjoy school or not it is well worthwhile gaining the best results possible at GCSE level. For some people this could mean A*s and, for others, much lower grades. Whichever it may be, gaining a personal best is a good indication to future employers that you would make a reliable member of the workforce and gives you a real sense of achievement.

If you are taking a post-16 course such as A-levels, AS levels, Vocational A-levels or a BTEC, but feel that it is not for you, you may be tempted to give it up and find a job. The best advice in this situation is to do nothing hasty and, again, to seek professional careers advice. Timing is an important issue. A few weeks into a new course and most people feel overwhelmed. Equally there is probably not a student anywhere, faced with A-levels only weeks away, who doesn't feel he or she has made the wrong decision.

Finding a job with a future

The world of work is changing rapidly. Like it or not every employer, no matter what the job, will look for good, reliable, enthusiastic employees with qualifications. Each year thousands of young people decide to pursue vocational training instead of taking a degree.

Learning as you earn can often be the best option. Working and going to a further education college, or doing a Modern Apprenticeship, for example, will ensure that you gain a qualification while earning some money.

All this means that you will succeed and get ahead in the world of work. I wish you luck!

Chris Banks
Chair, Young People's Learning Committee
Learning and Skills Council

Modern Apprenticeships

The most usual form of training for young people today is a Modern Apprenticeship, which leads to a National Vocational Qualification (NVQ) or Scottish Vocational Qualification (SVQ). NVQs (SVQs) are work based and practical. They show that a person can do a job well. Modern Apprenticeships also include Key Skills (Core Skills in Scotland) training in subjects such as teamworking, communication, information technology and problem solving – all subjects that help people to cope successfully in work.

A Modern Apprenticeship is a chance to have a job, be paid for it and gain a qualification, all at the same time. The training leads to all sorts of opportunities for promotion. Research has shown that in just a few years there will be over 9 million jobs for junior managers and technicians, and these are the types of jobs that will be filled by former Modern Apprentices.

Modern Apprenticeships are available in over 80 job areas, for young people aged between 16 and 24 who have the ability to gain a qualification while working. They are for men and women, for young people from all ethnic groups and for those who have disabilities. They come in two levels: Foundation Modern Apprenticeships, which lead to an NVQ (SVQ) Level 2, and Advanced Modern Apprenticeships leading to an NVQ (SVQ) Level 3. It is possible to move on from a Foundation

Modern Apprenticeship to an Advanced Modern
Apprenticeship and from there to further qualifications. In
Scotland Modern Apprenticeships are called Scottish Modern
Apprenticeships and in Wales they are called National
Traineeships and Modern Apprenticeships. For full information
about Modern Apprenticeships contact your local Learning
and Skills Council.

The way to get on to a Modern Apprenticeship is usually to
find a job with an employer who offers them. The job and the
training are linked. Some employers require GCSEs or
Scottish Standard grades at certain levels, while others select
Modern Apprentices through interviews and school records.
Most Modern Apprenticeships last for three to four years, but
individuals can work at their own pace and take a shorter or
longer time, as required.

Warning!

This book is only the beginning. It covers just a few of the
enormous number of jobs on offer. If it doesn't include your
particular area of interest don't assume that work and training
are not available. Ask questions, try your school careers
library, visit your local Connexions office – you'll be surprised
at the opportunities out there for somebody like you.

Work in administration 1

However large or small an operation, administrative work has to be done efficiently or the organisation will quickly collapse into chaos.

Job titles vary – secretary, administrative assistant, personal assistant or administration/office manager – but they all have certain things in common. Work is likely to include replying to correspondence and filing paperwork, organising and preparing for meetings, writing reports and dealing with phone calls.

Job opportunities

There are administrative opportunities in almost every type of organisation: hotels, schools, banks, factories, shops, hospitals, travel agencies, newspaper and television offices.

A few secretaries specialise in a particular type of work, for example they become farm secretaries, medical secretaries or legal secretaries.

The Civil Service, which is made up of separate departments and executive agencies, provides an enormous number of administrative jobs.

Skills and qualities needed

A good standard of written and spoken English is vital; so is an eye for detail, a good memory and a flair for organisation. Tact and discretion are important, as is being able to work as part of a team. Basic keyboard and word-processing skills are required for most jobs and some employers ask for shorthand qualifications.

5

Salaries

Rates of pay vary enormously, from around £190 a week to £346.

Ways into work

Foundation and Advanced Modern Apprenticeships in Business Administration offer an opportunity to gain an NVQ/SVQ Level 2 or 3. At present NVQs/SVQs are available at Levels 1–4.

If you are looking for a career in administration you can acquire basic qualifications in word processing, perhaps while at school, and then aim for a job in a company, which will provide you with training. With motivation and the right experience progression pathways for administrators can be impressive.

Alternatively you could take a secretarial course, for which entry qualifications are likely to be GCSE grades A–C, Scottish Standard grades 1–3 or equivalent qualifications. Courses usually last from one to two years and lead to qualifications such as:

★ City and Guilds Pitman Qualification Diploma;
★ Oxford, Cambridge and the Royal Society of Arts (OCR) Diploma and Higher Diploma in Administrative and Secretarial Procedures;
★ London Chamber of Commerce and Industry Examination Board (LCCIEB) Executive Secretary and Private Secretary's Diplomas.

These qualifications can be combined with a Vocational A-level (formerly Advanced GNVQ/GSVQ) in Business Studies or a BTEC HNC in Business and Finance.

The Civil Service

Administrative assistants are junior clerical staff. Each department and agency specifies the basic qualifications they require, which vary depending on the type and level of the job.

It is also possible to go in at junior management level. Minimum entry requirements are likely to be GCSE/Scottish Standard grades plus A-levels/Scottish Higher grades.

Specialist secretarial jobs

Medical secretary

The Association of Medical Secretaries, Practice Managers, Administrators and Receptionists (AMSPAR) offers a qualification for medical secretaries. Many colleges offer full-time or part-time courses lasting between one and two years, leading to the AMSPAR Diploma. Entry qualifications are four GCSEs grades A–C/Scottish Standard grades 1–3, plus a good standard of written and spoken English.

Legal secretary

People often work in legal practices with general secretarial qualifications. However there are specialist legal secretarial qualifications and many employers offer distance learning and part-time training opportunities to their staff.

A number of legal secretarial courses are available at colleges across the country. They include:

★ The Institute of Legal Executives Legal Secretaries' Certificate and Diploma (based on NVQs/SVQs);
★ The Institute of Paralegal Training – Legal Secretaries' Certificate and Diploma.

Entry requirements vary, but are likely to be a minimum of GCSE grades A–C/Scottish Standard grades 1–3.

Farm secretary

Rather than specialist qualifications, many farm secretaries possess knowledge of agriculture and general secretarial skills. Special training is available through part-time and correspondence courses and some agricultural colleges offer full-time specialist courses leading to:

National Certificate for Farm Secretaries. Entry requirements are three GCSEs grades A–C/Scottish Standard grades 1–3, a good standard of English and maths and some typing ability. Applicants must be over 17.

Finding a job

Information on Modern Apprenticeships is available from your local Learning and Skills Council. The Connexions service gives advice on careers in business and job opportunities locally.

Job vacancies are often advertised in the local press.

For information on college courses see individual prospectuses.

Case Study

Caroline Moyses
Medical Legal Secretary

Caroline's early ambition was to be a nurse. She studied sciences at college after leaving school, but then took the Association of Medical Secretaries, Practice Managers, Administrators and Receptionists (AMSPAR) Health Reception Certificate.

She found the course extremely interesting and says,

'I was in a good position because I'd studied sciences and learned keyboard skills at school, which meant I completed the course quite quickly. As well as covering secretarial and administrative subjects we also studied medical terminology so we could understand some of the technical terms we would come across in our future work.

'We looked at health promotion activities such as projects to persuade people to stop smoking, eat a balanced diet and exercise regularly. We also learned about patient care and ways of dealing with people who are agitated or upset.

'After finishing my course I took a three-month job with a medical practice and I'm still there.

'As medical legal secretary I deal with hospital referrals, sending out details of patients needing to see consultants and undergo investigations. The legal part of my work is largely working on insurance claims dealt with by the practice. Recent years have seen a big rise in the number of legal cases brought by people whose injury or illness may have been caused by negligence or some other reason. Such claims involve medical examinations and reports by doctors and I deal with the administrative side of this work.

'When the practice secretary is away I chase up appointments and carry out Health Authority work transferring medical records when patients move out of the area.

'I try to keep up with developments and at present I am completing the British Computer Society's European Computer Driving Licence. Whatever the job, keeping up with new training and qualifications is vital.'

Useful addresses

Association of Medical Secretaries, Practice Managers, Administrators and Receptionists
Tavistock House North
Tavistock Square
London WC1H 9LN
Tel: 020 7387 6005
Website: www.amspar.co.uk

City and Guilds
1 Giltspur Street
London EC1A 9DD
Tel: 020 7294 3505
Website: www.city-and-guilds.com

Council for Administration
18–20 Bromells Road
Clapham Common
London SW4 0BG
Tel: 020 7627 9876
Website: www.cfa.uk.com

Institute of Legal Executives
Kempston Manor
Kempston
Bedford MK42 7AB
Tel: 01234 841000
Website: www.ilex.org.uk

Publications

Questions and Answers Guide: Office Work, available from Trotman, £4.99.

Work in agriculture or horticulture 2

Over 1 million people in the UK work on the land or in jobs connected with it. The agricultural industry occupies 74 per cent of the country's land surface.

Farming has faced a time of difficulty and change recently. Farms today are becoming more competitive and introducing new working methods to balance the need for increased yields with environmental issues. While the production of food is still the main objective, farmers are diversifying, providing sport and leisure activities.

Some land-based industries, such as landscaping and horticulture, are expanding. If you are energetic, physically fit and enjoy being in the open air whatever the weather, there are interesting career opportunities with good prospects in this sector. The main job areas are:

★ agricultural engineering
★ agriculture
★ conservation
★ floristry
★ forestry/arboriculture
★ horticulture
★ landscaping.

Agricultural engineering

Modern agriculture involves the use of highly technical machinery. Agricultural engineers manufacture, develop, test and demonstrate new products and install, maintain and repair machinery on farms.

They design, make and install automatic control systems to provide the right environment for housed animals and for drying crops. There is also a thriving agricultural and garden machinery industry, selling and servicing machinery.

Job opportunities

These include service engineering and sales and marketing.

Skills and qualities needed

A fascination for machinery plus an interest in agriculture are needed, as is a practical approach to solving problems. It is important to get on well with both colleagues and customers. Computers play an important part in engineering, so developing IT skills is important.

Salaries

A skilled craftsman earns a minimum of around £210 per week.

Prospects

There are increasing opportunities for the right type of young person in manufacturing, testing, demonstrating, sales, maintenance and repairs.

Ways into work

Advanced and Foundation Modern Apprenticeships are available in Land-based Service Engineering (see Introduction) leading to an NVQ/SVQ at Level 2 or 3 in Service Engineering.

Colleges run courses such as the BTEC National Diploma course leading to the qualification of engineering technician. Entry requirements are four GCSEs A–C grades/Scottish Standard grades 1–3 or equivalent qualification.

Finding a job

See section on **Agriculture**.

Agriculture

UK farms range from small hill farms rearing beef cattle and pigs to enormous mechanised arable farms with no animals. The main farm types are dairy, beef, sheep, pigs, poultry, cereals, vegetables and non-food or industrial crops such as flax, lavender and pharmaceuticals.

Job opportunities

These include:

★ livestock production
★ crop production and management
★ poultry production
★ mixed farming
★ livestock management.

Skills and qualities needed

Agricultural workers need to enjoy working outdoors, have an interest in animals and plants and a flexible approach to work. They have to keep up with new developments and technology. While working as part of a team they will sometimes have to make decisions for themselves.

Salaries

An agricultural worker working a basic 39-hour week earns around £110 at 16 years, rising to around £180 for those aged over 19.

What can I do with... no degree?

Prospects

There are good opportunities for skilled people. With experience there is the possibility of moving into different job areas and of promotion.

Ways into work

Foundation and Advanced Modern Apprenticeships (see Introduction) are available in Agricultural Crops and Livestock. They lead to an NVQ/SVQ at Level 2 or Level 3. NVQs/SVQs at Levels 1 to 4 are available in:

★ agriculture
★ livestock production
★ extensive crop production
★ poultry production
★ mixed farming
★ livestock management
★ crop management.

Many colleges offer courses in:

★ **Foundation Agriculture** – no set entry qualifications;
★ **BTEC First Diploma** – no set entry qualifications;
★ **National Diploma** – entry requirements are four GCSEs A–C grades/Scottish Standard grades 1–3 or equivalent.

A list of land-based colleges is available from Lantra, the National Training Organisation for Land-based Industries (see Useful addresses).

Finding a job

For information about Modern Apprenticeships contact the local Learning and Skills Council. The Connexions service gives advice on Modern Apprenticeships and job opportunities. Jobs are often advertised in local newspapers and farmers can be contacted for possible job vacancies.

Conservation

Environment conservation is about making the best use of scientific knowledge, finding solutions that not only make best use of the environment for the present, but also for future generations. Locally it includes community recycling, planning and parks; nationally it covers pollution, roads and Areas of Outstanding Natural Beauty.

Job opportunities

The majority of work is in the conservation of landscapes, plants and animals in rural and urban environments and in the maintenance and conservation of rivers, coastlines and waterways.

Skills and qualities needed

The work requires an interest in and understanding of plants and natural life, an ability to work as part of a team and to plan and keep to schedules. It is varied and demands flexibility, enthusiasm and physical stamina. Tact is necessary, as members of the public may not always understand the value of the work.

Salaries

A trained park ranger can expect to earn in the region of £200 rising to £364 a week on promotion.

Prospects

The environment industry is growing in line with public interest, but it is a popular employment area and finding a job can be difficult. It is usually necessary to have been involved in work experience projects, before finding a job.

Ways into work

There are Advanced and Foundation Modern Apprenticeships in Environmental Conservation (see Introduction) leading to an NVQ/SVQ at Level 2 or 3 in Environmental Conservation available across the UK. NVQs/SVQs are available in Environment Conservation at Levels 1–4 with different specialisms at each level.

Environment conservation college courses include:

★ **Foundation Conservation** – no set qualifications required;
★ **First Diploma in Conservation and Forestry** – no set qualifications required;
★ **National Diploma in Countryside Management** – entry requirements are four GCSEs A–C grades/Scottish Standard grades 1–3.

Finding a job

See section on **Agriculture**. Jobs with training are often advertised in local papers.

Floristry

Floristry is the design and arrangement of floral displays for commercial customers. Displays vary from wedding bouquets and funeral wreaths to large arrangements for conferences and sporting events.

Job opportunities

The industry is largely made up of small businesses, linked together by relay organisations such as Interflora or Teleflorist. The small size of businesses means that everyone has to be prepared to undertake all types of work including sales, accounts, taking orders and stock control.

Skills and qualities needed

Florists need to have an interest in and understanding of flowers and plants and be creative, with an eye for colour. They have to work with other people and deal tactfully with customers both in the shop and on the phone. Florists aiming to run their own shops or to be self-employed need good business skills.

Salaries

A trained florist earns around £190 a week and an experienced florist around £280 a week.

Prospects

The floristry industry is expanding and the number of jobs in floristry outlets and garden centres is growing.

Ways into work

There are Advanced and Foundation Modern Apprenticeships in Floristry (see Introduction) leading to an NVQ/SVQ at Levels 2 or 3. NVQs/SVQs at Levels 2 and 3 are available in Floristry.

College courses lead to the following qualifications: First Diploma, National Diploma and Higher National Diploma, and the City and Guilds National Certificate in Professional Floristry.

Florists in work can take the Intermediate Certificate of the Society of Floristry and the industry's highest award – National Diploma of the Society of Floristry.

Finding a job

See section on **Agriculture**.

Jobs with training are often advertised in local papers and in trade papers such as *The Florist*.

Forestry and arboriculture

Forestry is the management of forests and woodlands. Arboriculture is the cultivating of trees and shrubs for amenity purposes, for example planting in parks, gardens and grass verges.

Job opportunities

In forestry these include:

★ establishing conifer plantations for timber production;
★ creating woodlands for leisure and game activities;
★ felling and transporting wood.

And in arboriculture:

★ establishing and maintaining trees and shrubs;
★ tree surgery;
★ designing landscape schemes;
★ managing tree care and planting contracts.

Skills and qualities needed

Forestry work requires physical fitness. The work is strenuous and often based in remote areas. An interest in plants and trees is essential, as is being able to make decisions and to work as part of a team.

Salaries

Wages in the forestry industry range from around £210 to £300 a week for a trained and experienced forester.

Prospects

There are only a few direct openings with the Forestry Commission or with private companies, but there are opportunities to become self-employed after training. In order to become a forestry supervisor or manager, a BTEC National Diploma in Forestry or an equivalent qualification is needed.

Ways into work

A Foundation Modern Apprenticeship is available in Arboriculture (see Introduction) leading to an NVQ/SVQ at Level 2.

Full-time or block release courses include:

★ **BTEC First Diploma** – no set qualifications.
★ **SCOTVEC National Certificate in Forestry and Woodlands**.

Entrance requirements are usually four GCSEs grades A–C/Scottish Standard grades 1–3 including Maths, Science and English.

Finding a job

See section on **Agriculture**.

Horticulture

Horticulture is the large-scale production and selling of plants, including fruit, vegetables, flowers, shrubs and trees, for food or decoration.

Job opportunities

Opportunities exist in garden centres and nurseries and at 'pick-your-own' centres.

Skills and qualities needed

Horticultural work needs knowledge of and interest in growing things from seeds or cuttings, the ability to solve problems and work in a team, plus an open mind towards new ideas and technology. The work often involves sales and dealing with customers.

Salaries

The starting wage for horticultural workers under 22 is likely to be around £140 a week. A skilled horticultural worker earns around £260 a week.

Prospects

Judging from the number of television programmes on the subject, gardening is highly popular. With over 18.5 million gardens in the UK there is a huge variety of opportunities in the industry.

Horticulture provides a vast range of opportunities for people of any age who with experience can gain promotion, move into new areas of work or set up their own business.

Ways into work

Foundation and Modern Apprenticeships are available leading to NVQs/SVQs at Levels 2 or 3 in General Horticulture, and Amenity Horticulture.

The Royal Horticultural Society (RHS) offers qualifications at General Certificate, Advanced Certificate and Diploma level. Colleges running these courses can be found on the RHS website (see Useful addresses).

Finding a job

See section on **Agriculture**. Jobs are advertised in local papers and in garden centres and nurseries.

Landscaping

The Wembley turf, gardens of a stately home, the central lobby of a shopping complex, the grounds of a new factory, or even motorway verges – they're all created and maintained by landscape workers.

Job opportunities

Most landscaping work is undertaken by contractors who tend to specialise in one area, such as:

★ domestic gardens
★ public areas
★ surroundings of commercial or industrial buildings
★ interior spaces of shops and offices
★ leisure facilities – golf courses and sports grounds.

Skills and qualities needed

Health and fitness are essential and so is an interest in plants and knowledge of the principles of design. Getting on with people and working as part of a team are important and this type of work involves being well organised and having a good sense of time management.

Salaries

Landscape designers are often self-employed and set their own rates of pay. Starting pay for a qualified landscape designer in full-time employment is likely to be around £211 a week.

Prospects

Opportunities in landscaping are increasing. The work varies, from employment with a big contractor working on large-scale maintenance or development projects, to small-scale garden design involving close contact with the customer.

Ways into work

There are Advanced and Foundation Modern Apprenticeships in Landscaping (see Introduction) leading to an NVQ/SVQ at Level 2 or 3. NVQs/SVQs are available at Levels 1–4.

Colleges offer courses leading to:

★ **BTEC First Diploma** – no set entry qualifications;
★ **National Diploma** – entry requirements are four GCSEs A–C grades/Scottish Standard grades 1–3;
★ **Higher National Diploma**, which requires one or more GCE A-levels or Scottish Highers.

Finding a job

See section on **Agriculture**. Jobs with training are often advertised in local papers and in the specialist publications *Horticulture Week* and *The Groundsman*. There are good opportunities abroad for people with UK qualifications.

Case Study

Steve Smith

Having grown up in the country, Steve know he didn't want an indoor job. From the age of 12 he had spent his weekends doing gardening for local people and was keen to make a career out of his hobby.

He went along to open days at Otley College of Horticulture and Agriculture in Suffolk and, after talking to staff about courses, opted to study for a one-year BTEC First Diploma course in Landscape Studies.

Afterwards Steve took a two-year National Diploma course in Horticulture, specialising in landscape and garden design.

He says,

'The courses were excellent. They were very practical and the teaching was great. During my time at Otley I did work experience regularly at a landscape design company and when I was coming to the end of my course they offered me a full-time job.

'There's much more to garden design than people think. At college we learned to draw plans and tackle the work in a professional way from start to finish. We undertake the whole job for customers – designing their gardens, soft landscaping, which is soil preparation, turfing and planting and hard landscaping, which includes digging footings, building walls, laying patios and putting in fencing and pergolas.

'It's the perfect job for practical people who enjoy working as part of a team. Eventually I would like to run my own landscaping business.'

Useful addresses

Lantra Connect
Lantra House
NAC
Kenilworth
Warwickshire CV8 2LG
Tel: 0845 707 8007
Website: www.lantra.co.uk

Agriculture

British Agricultural and Garden Machinery Association
Cardinal Point
Park Road
Rickmansworth
Herts WD3 1RE
Tel: 01923 432645
Website: www.bagma.com

Conservation

British Trust for Conservation Volunteers
Conservation Centre
163 Balby Road
Balby
Doncaster DN3 0RH
Tel: 01302 572244
Website: www.btcv.org

Floristry

The Society of Floristry
PO Box 561
Bristol
BS99 3ZW
Tel: 0870 241 0432
Website: www.societyoffloristry.org

Forestry and arboriculture

Lantra Connect
Lantra House
NAC
Kenilworth
Warwickshire CV8 2LG
Tel: 0845 707 8007
Website: www.lantra.co.uk

Horticulture

Institute of Horticulture
14/15 Belgrave Square
London SW1X 8PS
Tel: 020 7245 6943
Website: www.horticulture.org.uk

The Royal Horticultural Society
80 Vincent Square
London SW1P 2PE
Tel: 020 7834 4333
Website: www.rhs.org.uk

Landscaping

The Landscape Institute
6–8 Barnard Mews
London SW11 1QU
Tel: 020 7350 5200
Website: www.L-I.org.uk

Publications

Careers Working Outdoors, Kogan Page, £8.99.
Questions and Answers Careers Guide: Environment, Trotman, £4.99.
Real Life Guide to Working Outdoors, Trotman, £9.99.
Working in Agriculture and Horticulture, COIC, £5.50.

3 Work with animals

Today the British spend more money on their animals' health and appearance than ever before, and in many homes traditional pets such as cats and dogs have been joined by exotic species such as snakes, lizards and terrapins. The horse population is also on the increase, together with a growing interest in racing, showjumping and leisure riding. This has created more jobs working with animals and in support industries such as farriery (shoeing horses), saddlery and animal transport.

Details of the full range of opportunities for working with animals is available from the National Training Organisation for Land-based Industries, Lantra (see Useful addresses).

Job opportunities

The main job areas are as follows.

Animal care

★ boarding kennels and catteries
★ grooming parlours
★ pet shops
★ pharmaceutical companies
★ pet sitting
★ the RSPCA.

Equine industries

★ riding schools
★ hunt stables
★ competition stables

★ livery stables
★ trekking centres
★ riding holiday hotels
★ racing stables
★ stud farms.

Veterinary nursing

★ veterinary practices
★ laboratories
★ zoos
★ breeding and boarding kennels.

Animal care

Job opportunities

Grooming parlours

More and more owners are treating their pets to regular visits to grooming salons. Treatments include bathing, shampooing, drying, clipping, trimming and brushing both long- and short-haired dogs. Dog groomers also carry out specialist treatments such as nail clipping, teeth cleaning, ear care and treatment for parasites.

Pet shops

These range from large retail chains to small, family-owned businesses. As well as selling fish, birds and small animals such as guinea pigs and hamsters, pet shops usually sell food, bedding, cages and baskets. The job includes cleaning and feeding animals and checking they are healthy, serving customers and giving advice on animal care.

Kennels, catteries and pharmaceuticals

This involves feeding and exercising, checking the animals for illness, cleaning out quarters and changing bedding. Work varies according to the type of accommodation: breeding, boarding, quarantine, hunt, racing or those run by welfare organisations.

Openings exist for animal carers in pharmaceutical laboratories and research centres where animals are kept in a controlled environment for clinical testing.

Pet sitting

Instead of putting pets into kennels or catteries when the family goes on holiday, more and more people are arranging for experienced carers to move in and care for pets in their own homes.

The RSPCA

RSPCA inspectors provide 24-hour cover for animals in need. They investigate complaints of cruelty, carry out rescues, bring cases to court, inspect animal establishments, give advice and administer first aid.

Far more people apply for this work than there are training opportunities. Successful applicants need GCSEs in English language and a science subject. They undertake a tough six-month training course, which includes mountain and boat rescue techniques, court work and public speaking as well as animal welfare. There is a written exam followed by six months probationary work before the full qualification is awarded.

Skills and qualities needed

A love of animals is vital, but nobody working in animal care can afford to be sentimental. Patience is needed, plus the ability to handle animals firmly but kindly. The work can be messy and unpleasant and involves being outdoors in all types of weather, so physical and mental stamina are necessary. Contact with owners or potential owners is part of the job and customer care is important, as is a pleasant manner and good communication skills.

Salary

Job opportunities vary from area to area. Hours and rates of pay are negotiable but usually include weekend work. Starting pay is around £164 a week. Pet shop assistants work a 35 to 39 hour week, and most assistants earn between £177 and £254 a week. A skilled dog groomer whose work is in demand can earn up to £600 a week. There are also good opportunities for self-employment.

Prospects

With the right attitude and training there are opportunities to move into management, or to set up your own business.

Ways into Work

Animal care

Foundation and Advanced Modern Apprenticeships (see Introduction) are available in Animal Care for young people. They lead to an NVQ/SVQ at Level 2 or 3.

Colleges offer a variety of animal care courses, such as:

★ **Foundation Programme in Animal Care**

  ★ The course covers practical skills plus numeracy, literacy and communication. It can lead on to a First Diploma, NVQ Programme or Foundation Modern Apprenticeship. The main entry requirement is a passion for animals.

★ **First Diploma in Animal Care**

  ★ Entry requirements are likely to be GCSEs at grades A–D, Scottish Standard grades 1–4, in Maths and Science, plus a good basic education and a keen interest in animal care. The qualification leads to work in kennels, catteries, pet shops, zoos, or as a junior technician in pharmaceutical companies and universities.

★ National Diploma in Animal Care

★ Entry requirements are GCSEs at grades A–C or above, Scottish Standard grades 1–3 including English, Maths and Science. A list of colleges offering these courses is available from Lantra. There is a City and Guilds Certificate in Pet Store Management and the Pet Care Trust also runs a correspondence course in pet shop management.

Dog grooming

There is an NVQ/SVQ Level 2 available in Dog Grooming. The training recognised by the British Dog Groomers Association is the City and Guilds Dog Grooming Certificate 775 and the Advanced Grooming Diploma.

The RSPCA

The minimum age for trainees is 22. Applicants need GCSE grades A–C, Scottish Standard grades 1–3 in English Language and Science. They must be physically fit and strong swimmers.

Finding a job

For information about Modern Apprenticeships contact the local Learning and Skills Council. The Connexions service gives advice on Modern Apprenticeships and job opportunities.

Equine industries

Thousands of people earn their living working with horses as instructors, grooms, jockeys, farriers or in the many jobs connected with the industry such as equine insurance, transport or feed supplies.

Job opportunities

Riding instructor

Levels of instruction range from teaching children the basic techniques to coaching professionals. Stable and yard duties such as mucking out and cleaning equipment as well as exercising, grooming and feeding the horses are part of the job for all but the very top instructors.

Groom

This involves looking after valuable horses worth thousands of pounds, so grooms need to be well trained and competent. They are usually responsible for the day-to-day care of horses: inspecting them for injury, feeding, cleaning, brushing and trimming, mucking out and exercising. When a horse is ill or injured the groom provides nursing care, following the vet's instructions. There are opportunities for grooms in polo, horse trials, driving, dressage, showing, hunting and studs.

Racing

There are two types of horse racing: flat racing, which takes place from March to November; and National Hunt racing over jumps, which takes place all year round.

Stable and stud staff work is available in racing yards or in the thoroughbred breeding industry. Trainees who show riding potential may have a chance to train as a jockey. Jobs in the racing industry usually involve living away from home.

Skills and qualities needed

An affection for and interest in horses is essential. Almost all equine care involves riding horses, so workers need to become competent riders. The work is physically demanding, so good health is important too. Grooms need to have good hand–eye co-ordination, as some of the work such as plaiting and grooming for competitions can be intricate.

To teach riding demands patience and understanding and strong communication skills plus a liking for people as well as horses.

Salary

A qualified groom earns around £192 a week and a yard or stable manager, with responsibilities for running the operation, around £384 a week. A newly qualified riding instructor earns around £192 a week.

Prospects

Working with horses is a way of life. If you are prepared to work hard and cope with irregular hours there are good opportunities, including specialising in a particular type of work such as dressage or eventing, or taking on management responsibilities.

Ways into work

The British Horse Society (BHS) administers equine qualifications for work in the industry:

★ **BHS Horse Knowledge and Riding Stage Examinations 1–4.**
★ **Preliminary Teacher's Certificate** – to take the exam candidates need to have passed the Horse Knowledge and Riding examination at Stage 2. Candidates under 18 require four GCSE passes at grades A–C, Scottish Standard grades 1–3 including English (or an equivalent qualification).
★ **BHS Intermediate Instructor Certificate** – the main professional qualification for riding instructors. Candidates must be over 22.

Riding instruction and grooming

Foundation and Advanced Modern Apprenticeships (see Introduction) are available in Equine Care for young people. They lead to an NVQ/SVQ at Levels 1, 2 or 3. Candidates with an NVQ/SVQ at Levels 2 and 3 are eligible for direct entry to the BHS Stage Examinations.

The BHS publishes a book called *Where to Ride* (see Useful addresses).

The horse racing industry

Training is provided at:

★ British Racing School, Newmarket;
★ Northern Racing College, Doncaster; and
★ The National Stud.

Training is free and leads to an NVQ/SVQ at Levels 1–3 and a guaranteed job. No academic qualifications are required, nor is previous experience in riding or handling horses. Anyone under 19 years working in a racing yard must attend a training course at one of the establishments listed above.

Finding a job

See section on Animal care.

Jobs are also advertised in magazines such as *Horse and Hound*, *Horse & Pony* and *Sporting Life*.

Veterinary nursing

Veterinary nurses (VNs) work alongside vets caring for all types of sick animals and carry out minor surgery and diagnostic tests.

Job opportunities

There are over 5000 VNs working in veterinary practices, charity-run clinics, zoos, universities and research centres, and job numbers are increasing.

Skills and qualities needed

VNs need a strong interest in animals and in biology. Good hand–eye co-ordination is important in order to carry out animal handling and delicate treatments. Record keeping and booking appointments are usually part of the job and VNs need to be well organised and able to communicate well with people. Tact and patience are required when dealing with people who are worried or upset about their pets. VNs must be prepared to carry out messy jobs.

Salary

Rates of pay depend very much on the location and size of a practice. A qualified VN is likely to earn around £280 a week and a practice manager between £288 and £384 a week.

Prospects

Opportunities are growing in the UK and VNs can become head nurses and practice managers.

Ways into work

Entry requirements for training as a VN are five GCSE passes at Grade C or above, Scottish Standard grades 1–3, including English Language, Maths and a science subject (or two science subjects).

Candidates without these qualifications can take the British Veterinary Nursing Association (BVNA) Animal Nursing Assistant course. This is available by distance learning or college attendance. Trainees must be at least 16 and have been working in a veterinary practice for 9 months full time or 18 months part time.

Training as a VN usually takes two years and leads to an NVQ/SVQ at Levels 2 and 3. During this time trainees normally work in a veterinary practice and attend college on day release or block release.

Finding a job

For information about Modern Apprenticeships contact your local Learning and Skills Council. The Connexions service gives advice on Modern Apprenticeships and job opportunities.

Vacancies for VNs are advertised in the BVNA's journal *Veterinary Nursing* and in the veterinary journal *Veterinary Record*.

Case Study

Suzzanne France
Jockey

'I love the excitement of racing and I really want to win.'

As long as she can remember Suzzanne has been interested in horses and wanted to be a jockey. To help her achieve this ambition, her father wrote to several organisations in the racing industry asking for information about becoming a jockey. and he was put in touch with the British Racing School at Newmarket.

Suzzanne explains,

'To be a jockey you need to be under eight stone in weight. Luckily I'm small so that wasn't a problem. However most of the trainees on the course with me wanted to work with horses rather than become professional jockeys, so the weight limit didn't apply to them.

'The course in Newmarket lasted nine weeks and during that time we all lived together in a hostel. Each trainee had two horses to look after and every morning we mucked out their stables and exercised them. In the afternoon there were lectures on horse health and welfare. At the end of the course I returned home to Yorkshire with an NVQ Level 1 and got a job in a yard in Malton. I gained my NVQ Level 2 and when I was 19 years old I got my apprentice licence, which meant I could race professionally.

'I also gained my NVQ Level 3 in Racehorse Care and Management through the British Racing School when I was 21. I'm 23 years old now and my apprentice licence (which enables a rider to claim a weight allowance in a race) runs out in two years, or before that if I have 90 or more wins. So far I've had five wins this year and I am determined to do well.

'There's no problem being a female jockey, but you do need to be mentally strong and take the rough with the smooth. While most people working with horses don't race them, they still need to cope with being outdoors in all sorts of weather and working hard physically. If they can cope with that, it's a great life.'

Useful addresses

Lantra Connect
Lantra House
NAC
Kenilworth
Warwickshire CV8 2LG
Tel: 0845 707 8007
Website: www.lantra.co.uk

Animal care

British Dog Groomers' Association
Bedford Business Centre
170 Mile Road
Bedford MK42 9TW
Tel: 01234 273933
Website: www.petcare.co.uk

RSPCA Headquarters
Wilberforce Way
Southwater
Horsham
West Sussex RH13 9RS
Tel: 08700 101181
Website: www.rspca.org.uk

Equine

British Horse Society
Stoneleigh Deer Park
Kenilworth
Warwickshire CV8 2XZ
Tel: 01926 707700
Website: www.bhs.org.uk

British Racing School
Snailwell Road
Newmarket
Suffolk CB8 7NU
Tel: 01638 665103
Website: www.brs.org.uk

The National Stud
Newmarket
Suffolk
CB8 0XE
Tel 01638 663464
Website www.nationalstud.co.uk

Northern Racing College
The Stables
Rossington Hall
Great North Road
Doncaster DN11 0HN
Tel: 01302 861000
Website: www.northernracingcollege.co.uk

Veterinary nursing

British Veterinary Nursing Association
11 Shenval House
South Road
Harlow
Essex CM20 2BD
Tel: 01279 450567
Website: www.bvna.org.uk

Publications

Questions and Answers Career Guide: Animals, Trotman, £4.99.
Real Life Guide to Working Outdoors, Trotman, £9.99
Working with Animals, Kogan Page, £8.99.
Working with Animals, Connexions, £5.50.

4 Work in engineering, construction or manufacturing

Here are a wealth of practical hands-on jobs with high quality training and good career opportunities.

Gone are the days when working in a factory meant little possibility for promotion or career development. There is a real need for enthusiastic young people of both sexes and most employers are pleased to give them the career chances they are looking for.

Engineering

Engineering is the process of designing and making the machinery and products of everyday life. In a fast-changing world it is also about moving technology further and further forward.

Job opportunities

Today 1.8 million people in the UK work in engineering and there are plenty of good job opportunities. Engineering covers a wide range of different areas. Some of the main ones are:

★ manufacturing engineering – organising ways of changing raw materials into manufactured products;
★ control engineering – designing and making robots, switches, satellite tracking systems – the machines that run the modern world;
★ electronic engineering – working with electricity to control equipment such as computers, mobile phones, microprocessors and electric circuits;
★ electrical engineering – generating and supplying electricity from power stations, transformers, generators and cables;

* ★ chemical engineering – changing raw materials chemically, so they make useful products such as plastics, paints, medicines and fabrics;
* ★ mechanical engineering – working with all types of moving machinery;
* ★ marine engineering – designing and building sea transport;
* ★ civil and structural engineering – designing and building structures such as the Channel Tunnel.

Skills and qualities needed

Engineers need a practical, enquiring mind and a fascination for how things work. They also need to enjoy working as part of a team.

Salary

Pay levels vary a great deal from company to company. As a rough guide, an engineering technician earns around £480 a week and an incorporated engineer around £600 a week.

Prospects

There are great opportunities to gain a recognised engineering qualification and to continue training to whatever level you wish.

The Engineering Council awards the following qualifications:

* ★ **Engineering Technician** – to individuals with a Vocational A-level (formerly Advanced GNVQ), completion of a Modern Apprenticeship, BTEC National Certificate or Diploma or approved NVQ Level 3 and also to those who have a minimum of two years' approved training plus two years' experience in a responsible position.
* ★ **Incorporated Engineer** – to degree graduates, people with HND/C plus further learning, a minimum of two

years' approved training and two years' experience in a responsible position.

★ **Chartered Engineer** – some people who may have started as Modern Apprentices may go on to take a relevant degree that would enable them, with appropriate professional development, to obtain chartered status.

Many engineers move into management roles or into non-technical jobs such as marketing, sales or finance.

Ways into work

Advanced and Foundation Modern Apprenticeships are excellent ways of beginning an engineering career. The Foundation Modern Apprenticeship lasts around two years and leads to an NVQ/SVQ at least to Level 2. Entry requirements vary. Some employers ask for three to five GCSE/Scottish Standard grades while others look for interest and commitment rather than academic qualifications.

The Advanced Modern Apprenticeship leads to an NVQ/SVQ at Levels 3 or 4. It usually takes around three to four years to complete and involves both off- and on-the-job training with part-time academic study. Entry requirements are usually four GCSEs grades A–C/Scottish Standard grades 1–3 including Maths, English and a science such as Physics or Technology. Although not essential, a GCSE pass in a modern foreign language can be very helpful to an engineer. After completing an Advanced Modern Apprenticeship it is possible to go on to university and take a degree in engineering.

NVQs/SVQs are available at Levels 1–5.

For those wanting to study full time there is a wide choice of engineering courses on offer at colleges across the country. A good way to start is to study one of the more general courses, such as electrical and electronic engineering, mechanical engineering, manufacturing engineering, fabrication.

BTEC programmes (not in Scotland) can be studied full time or part time, sometimes at the same time as a Modern Apprenticeship. The work involves both practice and theory:

★ **BTEC First Certificate or Diploma** – may require GCSE/Scottish Standard grade passes in Maths and Science;
★ **BTEC National Certificate or Diploma** – entry requirements are likely to be four GCSEs at grades A–C, Scottish Standard grades 1–3;
★ **BTEC Higher National Diploma or Certificate** – requires National Certificate or Diploma or an equivalent qualification.

GNVQs in engineering are full-time school or college courses, with a high practical content:

★ **Part I** – studied at school between ages 14 and 16;
★ **Foundation** – equivalent to basic GCSE/Scottish Standard courses;
★ **Intermediate** – equivalent to five GCSEs A–C or Scottish Standard grades 1–3;
★ **Vocational A-levels** (formerly Advanced GNVQs) – entry requirements are GCSEs/Scottish Standard grades, Intermediate GNVQ or equivalent.

City and Guilds certificates are usually studied part time and are based on classroom learning and practical coursework.

Course requirements vary enormously and many colleges take a flexible approach, running their own internal aptitude tests and interviews. Anyone interested in studying engineering should contact local colleges to find out exactly what is on offer and the specific requirements for each course.

Finding a job

For information about Modern Apprenticeships contact the local Learning and Skills Council. The Connexions service has information about Modern Apprenticeships and local job opportunities. Approaching local companies about job and training opportunities is a good idea. Jobs are often advertised in local newspapers.

SEMTA, the Sector Skills Council for Science, Engineering and Manufacturing Technology Alliances, runs an Engineering Careers Information Service and a website (see Useful addresses).

Case Study

James Mayhew

'I talk to customers and find out what they need. Then I either design a machine especially for them, or adapt an existing model and design the electrical diagrams needed to run it. Once the work is finished I programme the machine and install it for the customer. My work takes me abroad a lot. Recently I've been in France, Germany, Taiwan and South America.'

Jim Mayhew is 26 years old and an international service technician with Fix-a-Form International Ltd, part of the Denny Bros Group. The company specialises in making machinery to produce high capacity information leaflets – the type found attached to coffee jars, giving information about competitions and promotions, or inside medicine packaging containing user instructions in several languages.

James's GCSE results were largely Ds and Es. He was keen to try a practical approach to work and joined the company as a trainee service technician. A few months later James's training was formalised with the offer of a Modern Apprenticeship.

In his words:

> 'As well as an NVQ Level 3 in Machining Processes, I went to college on day release and took a BTEC Higher National Certificate in mechatronics followed by a Higher National Diploma. I also took two computer-aided design courses at evening class.'

James sees his job as offering him plenty of interest and challenges in the future as the demand for the type of machine produced by his company grows. Eventually he would like to specialise in design.

Construction

The construction industry employs around 10 per cent of the UK workforce and covers not only the building of new homes, offices, hospitals, roads, tunnels and railways, but also repair, refurbishment and renovation work. Even when there is relatively little new building going on there is still work for skilled men and women in the industry.

Job opportunities

Full information about the wide range of craft and technician career opportunities is available from the Construction Industry Training Board (CITB) (see Useful addresses).

Skilled craft careers include:

- ★ bricklayer
- ★ carpenter and joiner
- ★ floor layer
- ★ glazier
- ★ painter
- ★ plasterer
- ★ plumber
- ★ roofer
- ★ scaffolder
- ★ stonemason.

Technicians are the people behind the action on a building site. Their work is specialised and covers many different roles, including:

★ building technicians – work is often divided between site and office, supervising operations, drawing up plans and documents;
★ civil engineering technicians work on site and in the office on constructing roads, bridges, tunnels and all types of civil engineering projects;
★ estimators cost out projects, putting together estimates for possible future work;
★ buyers negotiate the cost and delivery of materials needed for building projects;
★ plant engineering technicians buy, hire and organise construction plant and equipment used on site;
★ site engineering and surveying technicians measure and prepare the site for construction, interpreting specialist plans and drawings.

Skills and qualities needed

Craft personnel in the construction industry need to enjoy practical creative activities and must have an eye for detail. They often work as part of a team so have to get on well with people. Safety is an important issue and a mature attitude to work is essential.

Salary

Apprentice salaries start at just over £120 a week. A skilled craftsperson working in the construction industry earns in the region of £7.70 an hour and a technician earns around £400 a week.

Prospects

Opportunities in the construction industry are very good. Craftspeople can progress to supervisory and management posts and so can technicians. There are good openings for self-employment. Qualifications can lead to university and a construction-related degree.

Ways into work

Craft

The construction industry has a training scheme called the Construction Apprenticeship Scheme, open to all young people from 16 upwards. It complements the Modern Apprenticeship programme, lasts for around three years and leads to an NVQ/SVQ in a chosen occupation.

NVQs/SVQs are available in various areas of construction from Levels 1 to 5.

Technician

It is possible to train at craft level and use the qualification to move on to technician training. To start on the Building Industry Technical Training scheme straight from school, a minimum of four GCSEs at grades A–C or Scottish Standard grades 1–3, preferably including English, Maths and Science, is needed. It is also possible to begin training after A-levels or an equivalent course. Training leads to an NVQ/SVQ at Level 3 or 4.

If you do not have the required qualifications but want to enter technician-level training direct you can take a vocational qualification (at a college) such as:

★ **Intermediate GNVQ/GSVQ in Construction and the Built Environment**;
★ **Vocational A-level (formerly Advanced GNVQ)**;

What can I do with... no degree?

★ **BTEC National Diploma**;
★ **SCOTVEC National Certificate**.

Finding a job

For information about Modern Apprenticeships contact your local Learning & Skills Council. The Connexions service has information about Modern Apprenticeships and local job opportunities.

The CITB can help with work experience placements, site visits and careers material. It also helps to find employers for young people who wish to train. For more information about careers in construction, or to apply for an apprenticeship, visit www.bconstructive.co.uk.

Case Study

Matthew Dunlop

Aged 21, Matthew is already an assistant site manager on a large housing development in Docklands in London.

After taking his GCSEs he was unsure what to do and 'dithered' for a while, before becoming a Modern Apprentice with a specialist refurbishment company and taking an NVQ Level 1 in Bricklaying.

In September 2000 he transferred his Modern Apprenticeship to Barratt, the national building company, and went on to complete it and gain NVQ Levels 2 and 3. During that time he represented his college in a national bricklaying competition.

Matthew's managers at Barratt could see that he had both now talent and commitment and they signed him for a two-year day release Ordinary National Certificate (ONC) course in Site Management. He is well over halfway through the course and is working as an assistant to a senior site manager.

Matthew says,

> 'I'm quite an organised person and I like dealing with people. I like bricklaying but I am ambitious and keen to be a site manager.'

He is one of over 400 Modern Apprentices working for Barratt across the country, and his bosses say that if Matthew continues as he started he could work his way up to director level with the company.

Manufacturing

The list of goods produced by the manufacturing industry in the UK is enormous: from food and drink, paper and clothing, to aeroplanes, pharmaceuticals and chemicals. While some traditional industries, such as heavy shipbuilding, have declined, others such as high technology industries have flourished. The nature of the work has also changed as processes have become more automated. Today there are fewer jobs at unskilled or semi-skilled levels and more at technician and professional levels.

Job opportunities

Over 4 million people are employed in manufacturing industries, in jobs that include sales, marketing, goods inward, packing, machine operation, assembly, administration and accounts.

In engineering people are employed as production manager/controller, maintenance engineer, tool room worker, designer, quality control manager, laboratory technician, product researcher (see section on Engineering in this chapter).

Skills and qualities needed

Production operatives need to work quickly and methodically, be reliable workers, good timekeepers and team players.

47

Salary

A manufacturing operative earns approximately £275 a week and a quality control operator earns around £384 a week, or more.

Prospects

There are opportunities to train to craft or technician level and move into supervisory or management positions or into quality control, transport or distribution.

Ways into work

Production operative

There are no minimum entry requirements for this work, although some companies have their own aptitude tests and initial training. NVQs/SVQs are established in a large number of industries including food and drink, glass, plastics and rubber. Modern Apprenticeships are available in manufacturing.

Quality controller

The work varies from short visual checks to complicated laboratory tests using specialised equipment. Quality controllers carry out the tests and analyse them afterwards.

Entry requirements vary across different industries. There are no minimum entry requirements and some people enter quality control after working in production.

Some companies recruit school leavers into quality control and may look for four GCSEs grades A–C/Scottish Standard grades 1–3 including English, Maths and Science. Foundation and Advanced Modern Apprenticeships are available.

Industries with complex quality control systems often recruit people with higher qualifications such as A-levels, Scottish Higher grades, BTEC National or Higher National Awards or equivalent qualifications. Some require degrees.

Many quality control personnel study for the City and Guilds (7430) Certificate in Quality Assurance by day release, block release or evening courses. There are no entry requirements for this course.

The Institute of Quality Assurance runs Diploma and Advanced Diploma in Quality Assurance courses, for which there are no set entry requirements. Contact the Institute of Quality Assurance, 12 Grosvenor Crescent, London SW1X 7EE. Tel: 020 7245 6722, Website: www.iqa.org.

Finding a job

For information about Modern Apprenticeships contact the local Learning and Skills Council. The Connexions service has information about Modern Apprenticeships and local job opportunities.

See the local press for vacancies, or contact companies direct for information about jobs with training.

Useful addresses

Engineering

The Engineering Careers Information Service
Science, Engineering and Manufacturing Technology Alliance (SEMTA)
SEMTA House
14 Upton Road
Watford
Herts WD18 0JT
Freephone: 0800 282167
Website: www.enginuity.org.uk

Construction

Construction Industry Training Board
Belton Road Industrial Estate
20 Prince William Road
Loughborough
Leics LE11 5TB
Tel: 01509 610266
Website: www.citb.co.uk

SummitSkills
Sector Skills Council for electrotechnical, heating, ventilating, air conditioning, refrigeration and plumbing industries
Gear House
Saltmeadows Road
Gateshead NE8 3AH
Tel: 0191 490 3306
Website: www.summitskills.org.uk

Manufacturing

Improve Ltd
Sector Skills Council for food and drink industry
1 Green Street
London W1K 6RG
Tel: 020 7355 0830

Publications

Getting into Engineering, Trotman, £9.99.
Questions and Answers Career Guide: Engineering, Trotman, £4.99.
Real Life Guide to Carpentry and Cabinet-Making, Trotman, £9.99.
Real Life Guide to Construction, Trotman, £9.99.
Real Life Guide: Electrician, Trotman, £9.99.
Real Life Guide to the Motor Industry, Trotman, £9.99.
Real Life Guide to Plumbing, Trotman, £9.99.

Real Life Guide to Working Outdoors, Trotman, £9.99.
Working in Construction, Connexions, £6.00.
Working in Engineering, Connexions, £5.50.
Working in Manufacturing, Connexions, £6.00.

5 Work with figures or money

The old picture of people, mostly men in dark dusty suits, sitting for hours on end at a desk adding up figures is far from true today. Now banks and building societies are fast-moving places offering a range of different services to customers.

In recent years many companies and organisations have taken control of their own finances, which means there are opportunities for working with figures in schools, hospitals, shops and voluntary organisations as well as in commercial and industrial companies.

Accountancy

Job opportunities

Accounting technicians work for accounting practices, industry and commerce and in the public sector. They work at all levels from accounts clerk to finance manager. Some are self-employed.

Accounting technicians keep financial records, check invoices, tax returns and wages. They make sure payments are made promptly and advise on book-keeping, credit control and payroll systems. Working as part of an audit team they prepare and check figures for clients. Much of their work is similar to that done by accountants, although there are some jobs done by accountants that cannot be done by accounting technicians.

Skills and qualities needed

Accounting technicians need confidence with numbers, good IT skills, an eye for detail and an ability to work under pressure. Also important are teamwork, good communication skills and determination.

Salary

Rates of pay vary, but an accounting technician with a basic qualification can expect to earn around £211 a week and a fully qualified accounting technician from around £270 to £300 a week.

Prospects

An increasing number of organisations are taking responsibility for their own finances, which means more jobs for accounting technicians. In small organisations they are often the only trained financial staff. There are good opportunities for self-employment. Accounting technicians can study to become accountants. The accounting technician qualification gives exemption from part of accountancy training.

Ways into work

No formal academic qualifications are needed. Trainees must be over 16 and have a good standard of English and maths. Those with an A-level or Scottish Higher grade in Accounting or in two other subjects, BTEC National Diploma in Business and Finance, Advanced GNVQ in Business Studies, are exempt from part of the training.

Foundation and Advanced Modern Apprenticeships are available (see Introduction). Accounting technician qualifications are linked to NVQs/SVQs in Accounting.

Two organisations offer qualifications for accounting technicians: the Association of Accounting Technicians and the Association of Chartered Certified Accountants.

Finding a job

For information about Modern Apprenticeships contact your local Learning and Skills Council. The Connexions service has information about Modern Apprenticeships and local job opportunities (addresses in local telephone directories).

Job vacancies are also advertised in local newspapers and in *Accounting Technician*, the monthly journal of the Association of Accounting Technicians.

Case Study

Kevin Webber

'I did apply for university because that was what everyone else was doing, but I was half-hearted about it because I saw graduates with huge debts, struggling to find a decent job.

'For as long as I can remember I've enjoyed working with figures and I took A-levels in Maths, Computing and Technology.

'When I was at school I had a part-time job in a Safeway supermarket and after A-levels I worked there full time while I decided what to do. There were good prospects with the supermarket. After two years I was an assistant controller, but when I saw a job in the local paper for an accounts trainee with the Colne Housing Society, offering the chance to work and study at the same time, I applied.

'I got the job and spent a day a week for the next three years studying at college, gaining NVQs at Level 2, 3 and 4 and becoming a qualified Accounting Technician.

'At present I'm working for Puffa, the outdoor clothing company, as an assistant accountant. I'm studying in my own time for the Association of Chartered Certified Accountants exams and attend an evening class one night a week. It's hard work but the course is interesting and it certainly isn't all numbers. At the moment we're studying corporate business law, people management and information systems.

'In another three or four years I should be a qualified accountant. I'm ambitious and see a good career ahead, either working within a company or setting up my own practice.

'When I was at school my teachers expected me to go to university, because that's what people did. I'm glad I made my own decision. I've never regretted not having a degree. I have no debts, an interesting job and excellent prospects. Many graduates would like to be in that position.'

Banks and building societies

The roles of banks and building societies are changing rapidly. Today most offer 24-hour, seven days a week telephone, online or interactive television services. Building societies provide a wide range of financial services in addition to their traditional role of arranging mortgages. Customer relationship management is increasingly important as both banks and building societies seek to persuade customers to buy more services from them.

Banking can be separated into:

★ clearing, retail and private banking – providing services for private customers;
★ corporate and commercial banking – dealing with companies;
★ investment banking – involving investment management and advice.

Job opportunities

Information technology has had a huge effect on banks and building societies and a number of tasks have been moved from branches to call centres. But no matter how technologically advanced organisations become there will always be a need for some direct interaction with customers.

Bank officers or customer services assistants sell financial services and deal with customer accounts, issue travellers' cheques and buy and sell currency, and are the first people customers meet. They usually begin employment as clerks, working behind the scenes on administrative tasks before dealing with customers.

Skills and qualities needed

Anyone working in a bank needs to be good with figures and have strong communication skills. A smart appearance and businesslike manner are also important. Patience is essential and so is an eye for detail, a flair for selling, honesty and reliability.

Salary

Rates of pay vary, but a bank or building society clerk can expect to earn between £150 and £320 a week. Some companies offer staff mortgages and loans to employees at favourable rates.

Prospects

Promotion is based on performance. It can often mean a move to a different branch, which may mean relocation. A bank or building society assistant can progress to bank officer and to trainee manager and bank manager. To move into management the Diploma in Financial Services Management is needed.

Ways into work

There are no formal entry requirements, although many banks and building societies do ask for four GCSEs grades A–C, or Scottish Standard grades 1–3.

Foundation and Advanced Modern Apprenticeships are available (see Introduction), leading to NVQ/SVQ at Levels 2 or 3 in Providing Financial Services (Banks and Building Societies). Staff in banks and building societies may also be required to take formal Chartered Institute of Bankers (CIB)/Chartered Institute of Bankers in Scotland (CIOBS) modules or examinations.

Finding a job

For information about Modern Apprenticeships contact the local Learning and Skills Council. The Connexions service has information about Modern Apprenticeships and local job opportunities (addresses in local telephone directories).

Job vacancies are also advertised in local newspapers and careers information packs are available from banks and building societies.

Insurance

There are two main areas of insurance: life and general.

Life insurance

People insure themselves so that if they die their family has financial support. Life policies are also used to build up savings for retirement. Pension schemes come into this area of insurance, as do long-term investment contracts to pay for events such as retirement or children's education.

General insurance

This divides into two sections: personal and commercial; personal insurance deals with motor and household insurance and accident cover; commercial business provides companies and employers with insurance cover.

Job opportunities

Insurance is a major industry, employing over 350,000 people in the UK. Job openings include:

★ insurance clerk, providing clerical assistance;
★ insurance underwriter, issuing policies;
★ insurance broker, helping clients select and buy insurance policies;
★ financial adviser, bringing in new business and encouraging people to plan for the future;
★ insurance claims official, checking claims and deciding whether they should be paid;
★ insurance surveyor, assessing the degree of risk in a new insurance policy;
★ insurance loss adjuster, investigating claims independently to decide if they are valid;
★ risk manager, identifying risks, inspecting premises and equipment to identify areas that might lead to loss or damage.

Skills and qualities needed

Most insurance work involves contact with customers, so staff need to be smart, with a good business manner and good communication skills. The ability to sell is important in many jobs, as is quick, clear thinking and a high level of personal organisation. Much of the work involves working on computers so good IT skills are necessary, as is being able to work with others as part of a team.

Salary

Rates vary considerably, but average rates of weekly pay after two or three years in the job are:

★ £300 for a clerk
★ £384 for a claims official/an insurance broker/insurance surveyor

★ £400 plus commission for a financial adviser
★ £450 for an insurance loss adjuster
★ £650 for a risk manager.

Prospects

There are opportunities for staff to move into supervisory, team leader or management positions, as follows:

★ Insurance clerks and insurance claims officials who are prepared to take Chartered Insurance Institute (CII) exams can become underwriters, brokers and financial advisers.
★ Insurance brokers can move into risk management and loss adjustment.
★ Underwriters may specialise in a particular area such as marine, aviation insurance or reinsurance, or move into surveying.
★ Surveyors can move into underwriting or risk management.
★ Financial advisers can move into senior posts or into areas such as marketing.
★ Loss adjusters can move into specialist areas or into surveying or risk management.
★ Risk managers can become self-employed or specialise in an area such as health, or fire risks.

Ways into work

There are no formal qualifications required to work in insurance, although many companies do expect certain standards of education.

Foundation and Advanced Modern Apprenticeships are available (see Introduction) leading to NVQ/SVQ at Levels 2 or 3 in Insurance. NVQs/SVQs in Insurance are available at Levels 2, 3 and 4.

The following are typical qualifications that may be required by companies:

★ Insurance clerk – four GCSEs/Scottish Standard grades including Maths and English. Clerks are encouraged to take the Certificate in Insurance awarded by the CII and also the Certificate in Insurance Practice.

★ Insurance claims official – two or three A-levels, three or four Higher grades or an equivalent qualification. Many companies promote insurance clerks to this level. Claims officials are usually expected to study for CII exams.

★ Insurance broker – entry requirements are similar to those of a claims official. Brokers usually study for CII exams.

★ Underwriter – entry requirements are similar to those for brokers. Underwriters are expected to pass the Advanced Diploma exams of the CII.

★ Surveyor – A-levels or equivalent as above. Surveyors are expected to pass the Advanced Diploma exams of the CII.

★ Financial adviser – employers tend to look for mature entrants for this area of work and expect financial advisers to achieve professional qualifications awarded by the CII or to pass the Institute of Financial Services exams.

★ Loss adjuster – it is unusual for someone to go into loss adjustment straight from school. Qualifications are awarded by the Chartered Institute of Loss Adjusters (CILA).

★ Risk manager – many people go into risk management after working in other areas, although some companies do take on school leavers as junior technicians and move some of them on to risk management posts. Risk managers are expected to study for the Institute of Risk Management exams.

Major insurance employers

★ AXA
★ BUPA
★ Legal and General
★ Norwich Union
★ Prudential
★ Royal and Sun Alliance
★ Standard Life
★ Zurich Financial Services.

Finding a job

For information about Modern Apprenticeships contact the local Learning and Skills Council. The Connexions service has information about Modern Apprenticeships and local job opportunities (addresses in local telephone directories).

Job vacancies are also advertised in local newspapers and professional publications including *Financial Adviser, Money Management* and *Broker*.

Useful addresses

Association of Accounting Technicians
154 Clerkenwell Road
London EC1R 5AD
Tel: 020 7837 8600
Website: www.aat.co.uk

Association of Chartered Certified Accountants
64 Finnieston Square
Glasgow G3 8TD
Tel: 0141 582 2000
Website: www.accaglobal.com

Building Societies Association
3 Savile Row
London W1S 3PB
Tel: 020 7437 0655
Website: www.bsa.org.uk

Chartered Institute of Loss Adjusters
Peninsula House
36 Monument Street
London EC3R 8LJ
Tel: 020 7337 9960
Website: www.cila.co.uk

Chartered Insurance Institute
20 Aldermanbury
London EC2V 7HY
Tel: 020 7417 4415/6
Website: www.cii.co.uk

Institute of Financial Services
IFS House
4–9 Burgate Lane
Canterbury
Kent CT1 2XJ
Tel: 01227 818609
Website: www.ifslearning.com

Publications

Accountancy Uncovered, Trotman, £11.99.
Careers in Accountancy, Kogan Page, £8.99.
Getting into the City, Trotman, £9.99.
Questions and Answers Career Guide: Accountancy, Trotman,
  £4.99.
Working in the Money Business, Connexions, £5.50.

Work in hair or beauty 6

Today hair and beauty are closely linked to fashion, and many women change their hairstyle and make-up regularly in line with the latest trends.

The time has gone when men were content with a haircut every couple of months. Today a significant number are prepared to improve their appearance by having their hair cut, coloured and permed and by buying products such as skin lotion and perfume.

This growing interest in personal appearances, plus the development of new techniques and treatments in the hair and beauty industry, have led to a growing number of career opportunities.

Hair

Job opportunities

Hair stylist

In this job you would be shampooing, cutting, styling, colouring and perming hair.

Skills and qualities needed

Hairdressers need to be lively and outgoing and get on well with all types of people. You need to be good at working with your hands, be artistic, creative and interested in fashion. You should look smart and be physically strong enough to be on your feet all day.

Salary

A newly trained stylist earns around £192 a week. Top stylists can earn £576 and more.

Prospects

Opportunities are good for trained stylists. Once qualified they can go on to NVQ/SVQ Level 4 and become a manager or self-employed. They could also take specialist qualifications such as African-Caribbean hairdressing or men's barbering. Some stylists also train in make-up techniques and go into the fashion or film industry.

Ways into work

There are no formal qualifications required for entry to hairdressing. Foundation and Advanced Modern Apprenticeships are available (see Introduction) leading to NVQs/SVQs at Levels 2 and 3.

Many colleges offer full-time courses leading to NVQs/SVQs. These usually last for two years. Some colleges offer a joint hairdressing/beauty therapy course.

Finding a job

For information about Modern Apprenticeships contact the local Learning & Skills Council. The Connexions service has information about Modern Apprenticeships and local job opportunities. Job vacancies are also advertised in local newspapers.

Beauty

Job opportunities

Beauty therapist

Beauty therapists carry out treatments such as hair removal, lash and brow treatments, facial and body massage, electrical treatments.

Skills and qualities needed

Anyone working in the beauty industry needs to be friendly and pleasant, of smart appearance, able to get on well with colleagues and use cosmetics well. It also helps to have a good sales technique and some knowledge of human biology and chemistry.

Salary

A trained beauty therapist earns around £240 a week while a manager or someone owning their own salon can earn £385 or more.

Prospects

Beauty therapy is a growing business and most qualified beauty therapists can find work in salons, health clubs and hotels or on cruise ships. Promotion is possible by training in specialist treatments, and by moving to larger employers where there are management positions.

Ways into work

Advanced Modern Apprenticeships are available (see Introduction) leading to NVQ/SVQ Level 3.

The most usual way into beauty therapy is by a one or two year full-time college course leading to qualifications such as BTEC National Diploma or City and Guilds Certificate. Entry requirements vary but colleges may ask for three or four GCSEs A–C, Scottish Standard grades 1–3.

Finding a job

For information about Modern Apprenticeships contact the local Learning and Skills Council. The Connexions service has information about Modern Apprenticeships and local job opportunities. Job vacancies are also advertised in local newspapers.

Case Study

Sue Over

Sue owns two beauty salons and employs 26 staff. The salons are open from 8.00 am to 8.00 pm six days a week and offer a range of treatments from manicures and pedicures to hair removal, nail extensions, facials and waxing. Medical staff from a local private health clinic carry out Botox and Collagen treatments at the salons.

By the time she was 16 years old Sue knew she wanted to be a beauty therapist and chose to study human biology rather than biology. After the first year of an A-level course she left school to begin a two year beauty therapy course.

Sue explains,

'At the time there were fewer beauty therapy courses than today. When I was offered a place on a course I decided to take it rather than reapply and risk not gaining a place.

'I knew I wanted to work for myself and when I was trained I hired a room above a hair salon and paid the owners a percentage of my takings. My bank manager was very helpful and suggested I would do better to find premises of my own. He pointed out that they could be out of town because avoiding the congestion and parking fees in the town centre would be a bonus to clients.

'For the first few months I ran my salon alone and then took on four therapists. Soon we needed more space and I invested in a mobile van so we could carry out treatments in people's homes.

'Before too long I was looking for bigger premises, thinking that I would then close the first salon. However I realised that there was enough business for both salons and five years after the second salon opened I expanded the first to more than double its size.

'More and more people are having regular beauty treatments, which is great for business. However as treatments become more complex, the equipment needed to carry them out becomes more expensive to buy.'

Useful addresses

Freelance Hair and Beauty Federation
8 Willen Hall
Luton
Beds LU3 3XX
Website: www.fhbf.org.uk

Hair and Beauty Industry Authority
Fraser House
Nether Hall Road
Doncaster DN1 2PH
Tel: 01302 380000
Website: www.habia.org.uk

Hairdressing Council
12 David House
45 High Street
South Norwood
London SE26 6HJ
Website: www.haircouncil.org.uk

National Hairdressers' Federation
1 Abbey Court
Fraser Road
Priory Business Park
Bedford MK44 3WH
Website: www.nhfuk.com

World Federation of Hairdressing and Beauty Schools
PO Box 367
Coulsdon
Surrey CR5 2TP

Publications

Careers in Hairdressing and Beauty Therapy, Kogan Page,
£8.99.
Getting into Beauty Therapy, Trotman, £9.99.
Questions and Answers Career Guide: Hairdressing, Trotman,
£4.99.
Real Life Guide to Beauty Therapy, Trotman, £9.99.
Real Life Guide to Hairdressing, Trotman, £9.99.
Working in Beauty & Hairdressing, Connexions, £5.50.

Work in health or social care

Childcare

The role of childcare workers has changed greatly over the past 20 years. Today the training includes working in a range of different situations, together with other professionals, parents and families, to provide the best care and education for children.

Job opportunities

The trend for both parents to work means an increasing demand for pre-school childcare, before and after school and holiday clubs.

Childcare workers are employed as nursery nurses and nursery supervisors, pre-school leaders, crèche leaders, special educational needs support staff, nannies and childminders. The work is in nurseries, schools, family centres, hospitals, cruise liners and hotels.

Skills and qualities needed

Affection for children and an interest in their development is essential. The work demands concentration and an awareness of possible dangers, a sense of humour, a flexible approach and the imagination to stimulate and amuse children.

Salary

Rates of pay vary widely. A qualified nursery nurse earns around £240 a week.

Prospects

There are opportunities for promotion to supervisor and manager and for self-employment, setting up nurseries, playgroups and school clubs.

People with an NVQ/SVQ Level 4 qualification in Early Years Care and Education can train as teachers on the Registered Teacher Scheme.

Ways into work

Childcare qualifications include:

★ **CACHE (Council for Awards in Children's Care and Education) Diploma in Childcare and Education**. This used to be the Diploma in Nursery Nursing (NNEB). It takes two years full time and three years part time and is run by colleges across the country. Entry requirements are usually two GCSEs at grades A–C, Scottish Standard grades 1–3 including English Language.

★ **BTEC First Diploma in Caring** is a one year, full-time course that gives students without GCSEs access to the Diploma or National Diploma.

★ **BTEC National Diploma** is a two year full-time course that requires four GCSEs A–C, Scottish Standard grades 1–3. Students with this qualification can work in childcare, or move on to train as a teacher, nurse or social worker.

There are NVQs/SVQs in Caring for Children and Young People at Levels 2–4. Foundation and Modern Apprenticeships (see Introduction) are available leading to an NVQ/SVQ at Levels 2 or 3.

Finding a job

Information on Modern Apprenticeships is available from the local Learning and Skills Council. The Connexions service gives advice on careers in childcare and on job opportunities locally.

Posts are advertised in local papers and in *The Times Educational Supplement*, *Nursery World* and *The Lady*.

Case Study

Ryan Wakley

Aged 20, Ryan is in the final year of a two-year course leading to an NNEB childcare qualification.

In Year 10 when everyone was choosing work experience options Ryan chose to go into a school, partly because he liked young children and also because he wanted to find out what made teachers tick!

He enjoyed his work experience so much that he decided to go into a career in childcare and took a GNVQ at Intermediate Level in Health and Social Care, before going on to a course at his local college.

His aim is to work with children aged between three and five and he has already spent some time working in a pre-school nursery class. Once he is qualified Ryan sees himself working locally for a while before considering going further afield.

In his words:

> 'There are plenty of opportunities for travel with this qualification, so I'll see how I feel once I've found my feet. Meanwhile it's great working with young children and seeing them develop.'

Dental care

Job opportunities

Dental nurse

This job involves looking after patients, preparing equipment, mixing materials, updating records, sterilising instruments.

Dental technician

Dental technicians make up dental appliances such as braces, crowns, bridges and dentures from prescriptions written by dentists.

Skills and qualities needed

Dental nurses need to have a calm friendly manner and an understanding approach towards patients, including those who are tense and nervous. You must have good communication skills, a neat professional appearance, and be able to cope with difficult situations. An interest in biology is also important.

Dental technicians need an eye for detail. You have to be good with your hands and have an interest in science and technology, in order to keep up with continuing developments. Good communication skills and the ability to work with others are important.

Salary

A trained registered dental nurse earns around £250 a week, rising to around £390 a week.

Dental technicians earn a minimum of £256 when qualified.

Prospects

In dental hospitals and dental centres there are opportunities for dental nurses to reach senior positions. They can take further training in oral health education, dental anaesthetic nursing or become a hygienist. In hospitals or large dental practices there are management opportunities for dental nurses.

There is a promotional ladder for technicians leading to the position of chief dental technician in charge of a laboratory. In the commercial sector dental technicians can work at all levels and become self-employed.

Ways into Work

Dental nurse

Many dentists are willing to train dental nurses without formal entry requirements, although GCSE/Scottish Standard grades in English and Biology are helpful. Nurses training this way should study for the National Certificate for Dental Nurses run by many colleges as a part-time evening course. There are also full-time one or two year training courses run by colleges and hospitals. Entry requirements for these are usually two to four GCSEs at grades A–C, Scottish Standard grades 1–3, preferably including English language and Biology. NVQs/SVQs Levels 2 and 3 are available in Oral Healthcare Support.

Dental technician

The qualification for a dental technician is BTEC National Diploma in Science (Dental Technology), or the Scottish Vocational Educational Council (SCOTVEC) Diploma. The entry requirements are: four GCSE passes at Grade C and above, of which two should be in science subjects; or a BTEC first certificate in science, or an equivalent qualification.

There are three main training routes:

★ a training place within a commercial laboratory while attending a college of further education or technology one day a week, for up to five years;
★ a three year full-time course in dental technology;
★ a four year sandwich course within the NHS, where part of the time is spent at college and part at the laboratory.

Finding a job

Careers information is available from professional bodies (see under Useful addresses) and from Connexions offices. Job vacancies are often advertised in the local press and in *The Dental Technician* and *British Dental Nurses' Journal*.

Nursing

The National Health Service is the largest employer of nurses. As there is a current shortage, employment prospects are excellent.

Job opportunities

Nurses work in a variety of settings including doctors' surgeries, hospitals, hospices, health centres, patients' homes, schools and factories. Once trained as a registered nurse they can specialise in a wide range of jobs including psychiatric work, midwifery*, district nursing or operating theatre duties.

*NB students wishing to enter midwifery can either train as nurses and then take a shortened midwifery course or opt for direct entry midwifery training.

Skills and qualities needed

Nurses have to get on well with people of all ages and backgrounds. They need to be sensitive, understanding, well organised, practical and able to remain calm in a crisis. While working as part of a team they also need to be able to work alone.

Salary

The starting salary for a nurse in the NHS is around £317 a week. Nurses in the highest paid posts (as nurse consultants) earn around £926 a week.

Prospects

Employment prospects are very good. As well as working in the NHS, nurses are employed in private hospitals, nursing homes and in industry. There are opportunities for nurses to move into management nursing posts, to go into research or education. They can also take further training, to specialise in such areas as midwifery, mental health, district or children's nursing.

Ways into work

Students need to be 17 years six months to start training on the diploma course. Entry qualifications are five GCSEs (A–C), Scottish Standard grades 1–3 (English is required in Scotland) or an equivalent qualification such as NVQ/SVQ Level 3, AVCE/GSVQ. Diploma courses last for three years.

Students undertaking a diploma course will need to choose one of the four branches of nursing – Adult, Children, Mental Health and Learning Disabilities. All four branches require different types of people to work in them. There is considerable competition for entry into some branches of nursing. Applicants should check the situation with each higher education institution (HEI) directly before applying.

There are other ways to enter nurse training:

★ People already working as care assistants in the NHS may be able to undertake the National Vocational Qualification (NVQ) in Care at Level 3. This level can be accepted as the minimum educational requirement for the diploma programme.
★ There are a range of Access courses available for people who do not have the traditional entry requirements for either nursing or midwifery. These courses must be Quality Assurance Agency (QAA) approved. Successful completion of the course meets the entry requirements for both the degree and diploma programmes.
★ Foundation degrees/programmes are being developed which on successful completion normally allow a person on to the second year of either the diploma (or degree) nursing programme.

Most student nurses receive financial support during training.

Finding a job

During the second part of diploma training students spend a great deal of time on practical placements in a variety of healthcare settings. There is a heavy demand for trained nurses in all areas of the country. Jobs are advertised in sources such as *The Nursing Standard* and *The Nursing Times*. Many employers also advertise job vacancies on their own websites.

Case Study

Ben Bowers

Ben, who is dyslexic, left school with no ideas about a career and no qualifications. He went to college and took an Intermediate GNVQ in Business Studies and GCSEs in English and Maths and decided to go into retail.

In his words:

'For the next five years my one ambition was to have enough money to enjoy myself with my friends.'

As he got older Ben began to give his future some thought and wondered about joining the police. He became a special constable (voluntary policeman) in his spare time and as part of his work sometimes found himself inside a hospital. The more he saw the more he liked and eventually he took a job as a nursing auxiliary.

'Originally I thought I would gain the qualifications to train as a nurse through my work, but I realised this would take a long time, so I went back to college and took a year-long Access course studying psychology, sociology and human biology.

'I'm now 24 and in my second year of training in Cambridge, working towards the Registered Nursing Diploma. The course is 50 per cent practical, 50 per cent theory. I find nursing exciting and stimulating, although not without its difficult moments. My ambition is to specialise in neurology, dealing with problems affecting the central nervous system.'

Case Study

Eve Almond

Eve is a student nurse working for her Diploma in Nursing and specialising in mental health. She chose mental health nursing because she feels it offers a chance to form a closer relationship with patients than other types of nursing. Mental health nursing includes working in hospital and in the community, looking after patients of all ages including those with acute or serious illness and those with long-term problems.

Now in her final year, Eve is specialising in work with adolescents and her long-term plan is to do therapeutic work with young people.

It took Eve some time to discover that she wanted to take up nursing as a career. She explains,

'I started an A-level course, because I was quite good at graphics. I wasn't really interested in the course and dropped out after a year. To be honest I'm not sure the school noticed I'd gone.

'My mother was a health care assistant in a hospital and I joined her there because it was a convenient job and I wanted to save money and travel. I enjoyed the work and began to think seriously about nursing.

'I took four months off and travelled around the world, then came back and applied for a training place as a nurse in Brighton. Once I'd gained a place I went off again, this time to Canada where I worked as a volunteer on farming projects.

'It took me quite a while to adjust to the training course. After nine weeks of theory in the classroom, we were on the ward for ten weeks' nursing practice. The course is tough and it isn't for anyone who isn't committed to nursing. I have enjoyed it and I'm looking forward to a career working closely with young people.'

Ophthalmics

Job opportunities

One of the opportunities is as a dispensing optician – ordering prescriptions for spectacles and contact lenses from manufacturers, measuring patients and fitting spectacles and contact lenses, advising on style and types of spectacles.

Skills and qualities needed

An interest in science and the ability to handle scientific instruments are necessary, as are patience and good communication skills. An interest in fashion is important as spectacles have become a fashion item for many people.

Salary

A trained dispensing optician earns between £276 and £480 a week.

Prospects

There are good opportunities for promotion to management level and for specialisation. Dispensing opticians who go on to train as optometrists are exempt from certain parts of the course.

Ways into work

Dispensing opticians must pass the professional examinations of the Association of British Dispensing Opticians (ABDO). Entry requirements are five GCSEs A–C grades/Scottish Ordinary grades 1–4 including English, Maths and a science. An Access course is run by ABDO for candidates who do not have the entry requirements. Full- and part-time diploma courses are run at Anglia Polytechnic University and City College Islington.

Finding a job

Most dispensing opticians work in ophthalmic practices, which range from small independent businesses to national chains, although some are employed in the eye departments of hospitals. Jobs may be advertised locally or in professional journals such as *Dispensing Optics*.

Pharmacy technician

Pharmacy is concerned with the development, preparation and giving out or dispensing of medicines.

Job opportunities

Pharmacy technicians work in chemist shops, now known as community pharmacies, and in hospitals.

Community pharmacy technicians help pharmacists by assembling items listed on prescriptions, checking that the products match those on the list and labelling drugs with details of name, strength and dosage instructions. They keep records and check stock levels, ordering supplies where necessary.

Hospital pharmacy technicians work in a team under a hospital pharmacist. They dispense drugs, check supplies and place orders with pharmaceutical companies.

Industrial pharmacy technicians work in laboratories, assisting pharmacists in specialised areas such as research or clinical trials.

Skills and qualities needed

Pharmacy technicians need a strong interest in medicine and science and the ability to work methodically and accurately. They should enjoy working as part of a team and those dealing with the public need to be friendly, patient and sympathetic.

Salary

Rates of pay vary greatly depending on the location and size of the company. The average salary of a pharmacy technician is between £188 and £288 a week, rising to around £340 a week after a few years' experience.

Prospects

There are good promotion prospects for pharmacy technicians in hospitals, where large departments have opportunities for management responsibilities and for specialisation. There is also a growing demand for pharmacy technicians in the community.

Pharmacy technicians cannot become pharmacists without going to university, taking a four-year pharmacy degree and completing a one-year period of pre-registration training.

Ways into work

No formal qualifications are necessary but it is helpful to have studied science to GCSE/Scottish Standard level. Hospitals often look for four GCSEs A–C grades/Scottish Standard grades 1–3 including English, science and Maths.

The NVQ/SVQ Level 3 in Pharmacy Services is the qualification for pharmacy technicians. This qualification demands a great deal of underpinning knowledge as well as the usual NVQ requirements, and most trainees achieve this knowledge through studying for the BTEC/SQA Certificate in Pharmaceutical Studies.

Most pharmacy technicians train while on the job. Community technicians tend to train by distance learning and those in hospital on day release. The BTEC/SQA course takes from two to three years on a day release basis and can lead to entry to a Higher National course.

An Advanced Modern Apprenticeship (see Introduction) is available.

Finding a job

Information on Modern Apprenticeships is available from the Learning and Skills Council. The Connexions service gives advice on careers as a pharmacy technician and job opportunities locally. Jobs are also advertised in the local press and in *The Chemist and Druggist* and *The Pharmacy Journal*.

Useful addresses

Childcare

CACHE
Council for Awards in Children's Care and Education
8 Chequer Street
St Albans AL1 3XZ
Tel: 01727 847636
Website: www.cache.org.uk

National Child Minding Association (NCMA)
8 Masons Hill
Bromley
Kent BR2 9EY
Tel: 020 8464 6164
Website: www.ncma.org.uk

Professional Association of Nursery Nurses
2 St James Court
Friar Gate
Derby DE1 1BT
Tel: 01332 372337
Website: www.pat.org.uk

Scottish Childminding Association
Suite 3

7 Melville Terrace
Stirling FK8 2ND
Tel: 01786 445377
Website: www.childminding.org

Dental Care

British Association of Dental Nurses
11 Pharos Street
Fleetwood
Lancs FY7 6BG
Tel: 01253 778631
Website: www.badn.org.uk

British Dental Hygienists' Association
10 Vermuyden Way
Fen Drayton
Cambridge CB4 5TA
Email: informationofficer@bdha.org.uk
Website: www.bdha.org.uk

Nursing

NHS Careers
PO Box 376
Bristol
BS99 3EY
Tel: 0845 6060 655
Website: www.nhs.uk/careers

NHS Education for Scotland
Careers Information Service
22 Queen Square
Edinburgh EH2 1NT
Website: www.nbs.org.uk

Careers Advice
School of Nursing
Queen's University Belfast

1–3 College Park East
Belfast BT7 1NN
Department of Health Sciences
University of Ulster
Jordanstown
Newton Abbey BT37 0QB

Northern Ireland Practice and Education Council
Careers Advice
Centre House
79 Chichester Street
Belfast BT1 4JE

Royal College of Nursing
20 Cavendish Square
London W1G 0RN
Website: www.rcn.org.uk

Royal College of Midwives
15 Mansfield Street
London W1M 0BE
Website: www.rcm.org.uk

Ophthalmics

Association of British Dispensing Opticians
College of Education
Godmersham Park
Godmersham
Kent CT4 7DT
Tel: 01227 738829
Website: www.abdo.org.uk

Pharmacy Technician

The National Pharmaceutical Association
38–42 St Peter's Street
St Albans
Herts AL1 3NP

Tel: 01727 832161
Website: www.npa.co.uk

Publications

Careers in Medicine, Dentistry and Mental Health, Kogan Page,
£8.99.
Careers in Nursing and Related Professions, Kogan Page, £8.99.
Directory of Nursing and Midwifery Courses, Trotman, £15.99.
Getting into Childcare, Getting into Nursing and Midwifery.
Both available from Trotman, £9.99.
*Questions and Answers Career Guides: Nursing, Dentistry,
Childcare, Social Work*. All available from Trotman, £4.99.
Working in Nursing and Midwifery, Connexions, £5.50.
Working in Social Work, Connexions, £5.50.

Work in hospitality, travel and tourism or sport and leisure

8

Today people find they have more free time in which to relax and enjoy themselves than ever before, which is good news for all branches of hospitality, leisure and tourism – hotels, restaurants, sports and fitness centres, travel agents and tour operators.

Hospitality (food, drink and accommodation)

Job opportunities

Over 2 million people in the UK (over 7 per cent of the workforce) are employed in the hospitality industry, working in pubs, restaurants, school and hospital canteens, bed and breakfast accommodation, hotels and hostels.

Jobs include:

★ hotel manager
★ restaurant/catering manager
★ housekeeping manager
★ chef/cook
★ hotel receptionist.

Skills and qualities needed

Tact and patience are important when dealing with the public. Jobs in the hospitality industry often involve shift and weekend work, so flexibility and energy are needed. A lively but conscientious approach to the job is important and so is dealing with the unexpected.

Salary

Rates of pay vary greatly, from area to area and company to company:

★ A newly trained hotel manager can earn around £400 a week.
★ A trained restaurant manager earns around £400 a week.
★ A skilled chef earns around £290.
★ A hotel receptionist earns around £230.

Accommodation may be provided with some jobs.

Prospects

There are good promotion prospects up to management level for those who are prepared to work hard and to gain qualifications such as NVQs/SVQs, which are work based and can be taken while in full-time employment.

Ways into work

No formal qualifications are required to work in the hospitality industry. Foundation and Advanced Modern Apprenticeships are available (see Introduction) in five areas:

★ accommodation
★ chef
★ fast food
★ restaurant
★ pub

and lead to an NVQ/SVQ Levels 2 or 3. NVQs/SVQs are available from Level 1 to 4 in Catering and Hospitality.

Schools and colleges offer various hospitality and catering courses including GNVQ courses as follows:

★ **Foundation** – no entry qualifications required;
★ **Intermediate** – entry requirements are one or two GCSEs at grades A–D/Scottish Standard grades 1–4;
★ **Advanced GNVQ** (now known as Vocational A-level) – entry requirements are four GCSEs at grades A–C/Scottish Standard grades 1–3.

The Hotel and Catering International Management Association (HCIMA) awards an Advanced Certificate in Hospitality Studies. Entry requirements are four GCSEs or NVQ/SVQ Level 2. Study is part time for people working in the industry.

The British Institute of Innkeeping is the professional body of the licensed retail trade. It offers a range of management qualifications, from National Licensees' Certificate and Catering Management Certificate to the Wine Retail Certificate.

Finding a job

For information about Modern Apprenticeships contact the local Learning and Skills Council. The Connexions service has information about Modern Apprenticeships and local job opportunities. Approaching local outlets direct about job vacancies is a good idea. Jobs are also advertised in journals such as *Caterer and Hotelkeeper* and *Catering* and in local newspapers.

Case Study

Ben Handley

An appreciation of good food runs in Ben's family. His parents used to run the Lifeboat Inn at Thornham on the Norfolk coast. After GCSEs Ben joined them and worked in the kitchen for four years learning his trade. He also went to Norfolk City College on day release for the City and Guilds 7061 and 7062 courses and gained an NVQ in Catering.

87

At 19 Ben decided to gain further experience and did relief work around the country before going to Titchwell Manor in Norfolk as sous chef and then as head chef. When wanderlust got the better of him he set off for Australia and spent several months working in a restaurant in Melbourne. He says:

> 'I loved the blending of different food cultures – Thai, Chinese, Italian, French.'

Ben is now head chef at the White Horse in Brancaster Staithe on the North Norfolk coast. It is a job that gives him ample opportunity to experiment with Mediterranean-type fish dishes, which he loves.

In his words,

> 'You're always learning and experimenting when you're a chef, which is great. Eventually when I've learned enough, I'd like to open my own restaurant.'

Sport and leisure

Sport and recreation are great ways to unwind and relax and in recent years there have been plenty of government initiatives encouraging people to lead a healthier lifestyle. There is no age limit to physical activities. Children from around 2 years old enjoy pre-school play and exercise groups, while many retired people belong to swimming clubs and keep fit classes.

Very few people reach professional status in a particular sport. The vast majority are simply enthusiastic amateurs, who enjoy themselves whatever the standard they achieve, and value the chance to get out, keep fit and meet people.

Job opportunities

Career opportunities in the sport and leisure industry include working in the following areas:

★ sport and recreation – leisure centres, stadiums and arenas, sports clubs, professional sport, development and administration;
★ health and fitness – health and leisure clubs, gyms, fitness suites in hotels and holiday complexes;
★ the outdoors – education and training, activity centres, sports (such as water sports);
★ children's play – out of school clubs, adventure playgrounds, play buses;
★ leisure parks and attractions.

Skills and qualities

Energy and enthusiasm are important, and so is an interest in sport at all levels, the ability to motivate people of all ages and work as part of a team. Good communication skills, both written and spoken, are important. A mature, responsible attitude to safety matters is essential.

Salary

A leisure centre attendant earns in the region of £206 a week.

Prospects

There are good opportunities for promotion to supervisory and management levels. It is considered important for all entrants to gain experience at a day-to-day working level before moving to senior positions.

Ways into work

There are both vocational and academic routes into sport and leisure including GCSE courses in physical education, AS or A-levels in sport and physical education and Vocational A-levels (formerly Advanced GNVQs) in leisure and recreation. Such qualifications can lead to job opportunities or to higher education courses. Practical qualifications in first aid or lifeguarding are also helpful when looking for a job.

Foundation and Advanced Modern Apprenticeships leading to an NVQ/SVQ at Levels 2 or 3 are available (see Introduction). There are NVQs/SVQs in Sport and Recreation from Levels 1 to 4.

Finding a job

For information about Modern Apprenticeships contact the local Learning and Skills Council. The Connexions service has information about Modern Apprenticeships and local job opportunities.

One step into full-time work is through part-time or voluntary work with an organisation. Details of centres approved to deliver NVQs/SVQs can be found on SkillsActive, the Sector Skills Council for Active Leisure and Learning website www.skillsactive.com.

Travel and tourism

Travel and tourism employs 1.6 million people and is the UK's fastest growing industry.

Visitors from abroad are drawn to the UK by its varied scenery and historical buildings and traditions. A growing number of British people take short breaks in other parts of the country, in cities such as London, York and Edinburgh and in scenic areas such as the Lake District, Cornwall or the Scottish Highlands. As well as taking breaks in this country more people than ever are leaving the UK for holidays in places such as Spain, France and Greece and further afield in the Far East and the US.

Job opportunities

Leisure travel agent or consultant

This is work in a travel agency, finding out what customers want, advising on resorts and travel arrangements, selling airline tickets, arranging car hire, booking holidays using a computerised system, advising on visas, inoculations, insurance, foreign currency.

Courier/resort representative

A 'rep' makes sure all runs smoothly and that visitors enjoy their holiday. They either travel with holidaymakers or greet them at their holiday destination. They answer enquiries, give information about the resort, organise trips and activities and deal with emergencies such as lost luggage or illness.

Skills and qualities needed

Both travel agents and couriers/resort representatives need to be sociable and like working with people. Tact and patience are essential and so is quick thinking and having a smart professional appearance.

Holiday bookings are done by computer, so IT skills for agents and consultants are important, as is a good standard of writing and numerical skills.

Not all couriers/resort representatives speak the language of the country they are working in, but fluency in a foreign language is a great asset.

Salary

A trained travel consultant can earn between £154 and £250 a week. An experienced travel consultant dealing in a specialised area such as business travel can earn up to £307 a week. Travel consultants usually get discounts on their own holidays.

A courier/resort representative usually receives free accommodation and meals and earns between £90 and £190 a week, depending on experience.

Prospects

Most couriers or representatives work short term on a fixed contract for a season, although the growing popularity of winter holiday destinations means there are some opportunities for working all year round. Most people spend a few seasons working as couriers/resort representatives and then move on to other work. With large travel companies there are openings for tour managers and courier supervisors.

For travel consultants working with large companies there are good promotion opportunities to manager and area manager and openings in tourist information centres.

Ways into work

Travel agent/consultant
A good standard of education is needed and some employers ask particularly for GCSE grades A–C, Scottish Standard grades 1–3 in English and Maths.

Most young people go into the work through the Modern Apprenticeship programmes, which lead to an NVQ/SVQ Levels 2 or 3 and Key Skills (see Introduction). There are NVQs/SVQs Levels 2, 3 and 4 and many large companies run their own training programmes.

Many colleges run travel and tourism courses including GNVQs/GSVQs, Foundation, Intermediate and Advanced (now known as Vocational A-level).

There are also BTEC/SQA Higher National Certificates and Diploma courses in travel and tourism. Entry requirements are A-level or Higher grades, plus GCSE A–C grades/Scottish Standard grades 1–3 or equivalent qualifications.

Courier/resort representative
Most couriers need to be over the age of 18. Companies look for people who have experience working with the public and abroad.

Some ask for GCSE grades A–C, Scottish Standard grades 1–3 in English, and Maths. Knowledge of a foreign language, even without a formal qualification, is a good selling point.

Some couriers/resort representatives take a travel and tourism qualification and the Modern Apprenticeship programme is also used by some of the large companies (see under Travel agent/consultant). Companies run induction courses to prepare couriers/resort representatives for the work they will be doing and the problems they are likely to meet. Couriers can work towards NVQs/SVQs at Levels 2 and 3 in Travel Services.

Finding a job

To apply for a job as a travel courier/resort representative, contact travel companies at least six months in advance of the season. Such jobs are very popular and companies often don't need to advertise. When they do they use national newspapers and trade publications such as *Overseas Jobs Express*, and *Travel Weekly*.

For information about Modern Apprenticeships contact the local Learning and Skills Council. The Connexions service has information about Modern Apprenticeships and local job opportunities.

Case Study

Sarah Chapman

Sarah is 26 years old and assistant manager of a travel agency.

'I left school after GCSEs and started an NVQ in Childcare. I gave it up to work in a nursing home because I was thinking of becoming a nurse, but the job didn't work out and I took an NVQ Level 2 in Business Administration. When I finished the training I found a job in a travel agency and throroughly enjoyed it.

'During the next five years with the company I gained an NVQ at Levels 2 and 3 in Travel and Tourism. My next job was assistant manager with a larger agency, and that is where I am now.

'When the manager is absent I am responsible for running the agency, looking after the administration and checking all is well with staff and customers. I'm qualified to work in the foreign exchange section and I also dress the windows, making sure the information is up to date and attractive.

'We're busy throughout the year, but our most hectic times are January and February when people are tired of the winter and want to look forward to a break in the sun. July and August are also busy when those who haven't booked a holiday want a last-minute bargain. Some people take brochures away and work out for themselves what they want. But many of them need help to find their dream holiday. Staff also organise tailor-made holidays for customers who want to plan their own holiday route, possibly travelling across several countries, and they need us to organise hotels and flights for them.

'I am working on day release towards my NVQ Level 4 and this involves quite a long journey to the training centre.

'To enjoy my job you need to be able to put people at their ease, chatting to them and being enthusiastic about their plans.

'The hours are long in the travel industry. I work most weekends and in January and February the agency is open on a Sunday. The pay isn't amazing but there are perks. I've just returned from a week's educational cruise and staff do have discounted holidays.'

Useful addresses

Hospitality

The British Institute of Innkeeping
Wessex House

80 Park Street
Camberley
Surrey GU15 3PT
Tel: 01276 684449
Website: www.bii.org

Hospitality Training Foundation
Third Floor
International House
High Street
Ealing
London W5 5DB
Tel: 020 8579 2400
Website: www.htf.org.uk

Hotel and Catering International Management Association
(HCIMA)
Trinity Court
34 West Street
Sutton
Surrey SN1 1SH
Tel: 08700 106689
Website: www.hcima.org.uk

Sport and leisure

Institute of Leisure and Amenity Management
ILAM House
Lower Basildon
Reading RG8 9NE
Tel: 01491 874800
Website: www.ilam.co.uk

Sports Coach UK
114 Cardigan Road
Headingley
Leeds LS6 3BJ
Tel: 01132 744802
Website: www.sportscoachuk.org

SkillsActive, the Sector Skills Council for Active Leisure and
Learning
Castlewood House
77–91 New Oxford Street
London WC1A 1PX
Tel: 020 7632 2000
Website: www.skillsactive.com

Travel and tourism

Springboard UK
3 Denmark Street
London WC2H 8LP
Tel: 020 7497 8654
Website: www.springboarduk.org.uk

Publications

Careers in Sport, Kogan Page, £8.99.
Careers in the Travel Industry, Kogan Page, £8.99.
Getting into Sport and Leisure, Trotman, £9.99.
Questions & Answers Career Guides: Sport, Tourism. Both
    available from Trotman, £4.99.
Real Life Guide to Catering, Trotman, £9.99.
Working in Hotels and Catering, Connexions, £5.00.
Working in Sport and Fitness, Connexions, £5.50.
Working in Travel and Tourism, Connexions, £6.00.

Work in IT, science or photography 9

Forty years ago there were only six computers in the world. Today there is scarcely an organisation anywhere in the UK that does not rely on information technology in some form or other.

Restaurants and pubs run stock control systems and order supplies online, insurance companies and banks keep customer account details on computer databases, newspapers and magazines are designed on-screen and town planners use computer programs to develop traffic flow systems.

The widespread use of computers means great job opportunities, not only with IT companies but with manufacturing, retail and travel operations, voluntary organisations, universities and hospitals.

More than 1 million people work as IT professionals in the UK, with just under half being employed in the IT industry itself. To keep up with demand and new developments around 150,000 to 200,000 additional professionals are required every year, so there are plenty of opportunities for the right person.

IT

Job opportunities

IT is a fast-moving industry, which means job openings are constantly changing and developing. Jobs include sales and customer service, teaching people how to use computers, entering data and developing software and hardware systems. Jobs fall roughly into four groups:

★ IT operations
★ IT services
★ IT sales and marketing
★ IT research and development.

IT operations

Large organisations run their own IT systems, supported by their own specialist IT operations department. Activities include helping staff members with computer problems, making sure the systems run efficiently, upgrading systems and deciding future developments to meet the changing needs of the organisation.

Jobs in IT operations include:

★ VDU operator – entering data and word processing
★ applications programmer
★ systems analyst
★ network manager
★ database administrator.

IT services

Many companies do not have their own specialist IT department. Instead they buy in the services of a specialist company and contract it to do the work. Even companies with a specialist IT department may contract in an IT services company for specific tasks. Typical customers could be a hotel wanting a new website in order to attract more visitors, a gas company wishing to make sure its emergency call system is up and running efficiently or a hospital investing in a new patient database.

IT service companies vary enormously and offer a wide range of activities: developing websites, designing and installing IT systems, looking after customers' problems with both software and hardware and managing particular projects.

Job opportunities include:

★ helpdesk operator
★ IT consultant
★ project manager
★ technical architect
★ software support professional
★ hardware engineer.

IT sales and marketing

Individuals and organisations are constantly upgrading their systems and buying new software packages. This provides great opportunities for individuals with both sales skills and technical knowledge. They visit potential customers to introduce their company's products and services. They listen to a customer's requirements and discuss how these could be met.

The work involves calculating exactly what IT solution a customer needs, writing out proposals explaining recommendations and the reasons for making them and negotiating the sales contract with the customer.

Job opportunities include:

★ client manager
★ technical sales specialist
★ marketing professional.

IT research and development

The challenge to develop new products is huge. Workers in research and development try to predict future trends across the industry and new software and hardware solutions. The work includes developing new products, testing new features, recognising and correcting faults before a product is on the market and writing user instruction manuals for new products.

What can I do with... no degree?

Typical jobs are:

★ software developer
★ product tester
★ technical author.

Skills and qualities needed

The idea that computer specialists are strange, lonely
individuals wearing anoraks couldn't be further from the truth.
A fascination for computers goes without saying, but IT
specialists also need to be good communicators, able to
explain technical matters simply, enjoy solving problems and
working as part of a team.

Salary

Salaries vary enormously from company to company and from
area to area. A computer operator with word-processing and
database skills is likely to earn in the region of £290 a week. A
helpdesk operator earns around £269 a week while a systems
analyst is paid anything between approximately £384 and
£769 a week.

Prospects

There are plenty of opportunities for progression in IT for
those who are prepared to work hard and keep up to date
with new developments. Promotion to senior and
management posts can be rapid.

Although there are openings for IT specialists in every part of
the country the highest number of jobs are found in London
and the South East. Working abroad is a possibility for
someone with the right qualifications and experience. A
significant number of employers in the UK and Europe
continue to need skilled IT employees.

Major IT employers

★ Microsoft
★ IBM
★ Oracle
★ Vodafone.

Banks and insurance companies, retail organisations, food and drink distributors, manufacturers, hospitals, in fact most sizeable operations in the UK have openings for IT specialists.

Ways into work

Foundation and Advanced Modern Apprenticeships (see Introduction) are available for young people in three IT areas:

★ using IT
★ IT and electronic services (installing, maintaining and supporting computer systems)
★ developing IT.

There are NVQs at Levels 1–4 in IT-related subjects.

BTEC First and National Diploma and Certificate courses in computer science or information technology, art and design or media communication and product (for those interested in computerised or website design) are run at many local colleges. Entry requirements are usually four GCSEs (A–C grades)/Scottish Standard grades 1–3.

Vocational A-levels and GNVQs/GSVQs in information technology or in art and design for those interested in computerised or website design are offered at many schools and colleges.

Finding a job

For information about Modern Apprenticeships contact the local Learning and Skills Council. The Connexions service has information about Modern Apprenticeships and job opportunities.

IT jobs with training are often advertised in local newspapers.

Case Study

Tom Sewell

Tom is a service engineer in the IT department of a county council. He is 19 years old and joined the organisation as a Modern Apprentice when he was 17.

'I work in a team of 17 people and together we look after the computer systems for the entire council. Calls come through from the helpdesk and are entered into a logging system. A couple of people in the team are responsible for allocating jobs. In some cases this involves travel to different offices across the county. I'm hoping to pass my driving test very soon, which means I will be able to go out on such calls.

'There are thousands of computer users looking to us for help. The most common problem is users forgetting their password. This can be put right from our desks, but first we have to carry out security checks to confirm the request is genuine and the callers are who they say they are.

'Computers have fascinated me since I was around 5 years old. I spent a year in the sixth form studying for a GNVQ in business and then joined the council. Several months into my Modern Apprenticeship I became fully employed, which meant I started to earn good money. I shall finish my apprenticeship in a few months and I am already qualified to work on Microsoft systems.

'The most satisfying part of my job is tackling a problem and being able to put it right.'

Science

Science is about using logical thought to examine a problem. From this examination come possible solutions, which are then tested by setting up experiments to see whether they are right or wrong. People working in science today are involved in curing disease, improving technology and making the world a safer, more pleasant place.

Job opportunities

Science technicians usually work in labs and workshops under the direction of scientists. They check and operate equipment, prepare specimens, perform experiments, prepare data and record and present results. They usually specialise in one particular area of science, such as nutrition, biochemistry or satellite technology.

Skills and qualities

Anyone working in science needs to be interested in problem solving and be able to think logically. They need a clear eye for detail and the ability to work methodically and accurately. It is important to handle equipment deftly and to have good communication skills, both spoken and written.

Salary

Rates of pay vary enormously with different companies and in different areas. A trained technician's salary is likely to be around £250 a week. The figure rises to around £403 a week, with technicians in management positions earning even more.

Prospects

There are good opportunities for technicians, many of whom work for large organisations where there are openings for management posts and for specialisation.

Major employers

These include research companies, government departments, universities, hospitals, public health laboratories, gas and electricity companies.

Ways into work

Employers usually ask for a minimum of four GCSEs grades A–C/Scottish Standard grades 1–3 in English, Maths and two sciences for technician posts. Laboratory assistant or attendant posts that tend to involve more routine work may require a Foundation GNVQ/GSVQ or a good general education and practical skills.

One way into a career in science is through a Modern Apprenticeship (see Introduction).

Foundation Modern Apprenticeships leading to an NVQ/SVQ Level 2 include:

★ food and drinks manufacturing operations
★ glass industry
★ health and social care
★ surface coatings industry
★ steel industry
★ water industry
★ optical manufacturing technology.

Advanced Modern Apprenticeships leading to NVQ Level 3 include all of the above, plus:

★ carpet manufacture
★ chemical sector
★ engineering maintenance or laboratory operations
★ gas industry
★ synthetic fibres
★ paper manufacturing
★ polymers
★ optical manufacturing technology
★ pharmacy technology
★ laboratory technology in education.

More are being developed. NVQs/SVQs are available in many scientific areas at Levels 1–5.

There are GNVQ courses at three levels offered by schools and colleges:

★ **Foundation** – a one-year course for students with no GCSEs/Standard grades, or with mainly grades F or G.
★ **Intermediate** – one-year courses for students with GCSE grades D/Standard grades 4.
★ **Vocational A-level** – one or two years for students with GCSEs grades A–C, Standard grades 1–3.

BTEC/SQA National Diploma, Higher National Diploma and Higher National Certificate are also available in science subjects.

The professional body for science technicians is the Institute of Science Technology. It has its own qualifications: the Ordinary Diploma and Certificate and the Higher Diploma. It also offers its own vocational qualifications at preliminary and core levels through a number of registered centres.

Affiliate membership is open to anyone working or studying in science technology at NVQ/SVQ Level 1, at the Institute's Preliminary Vocational level (see below) or for an equivalent qualification.

Associate membership is open to those who hold an NVQ/SVQ Level 2 or have the Institute's Core Vocational Qualification.

Membership is awarded to applicants with an approved qualification such as NVQ/SVQ Level 3, a degree, HNC or HND.

Finding a job

For information about Modern Apprenticeships contact the local Learning and Skills Council or the Science, Technology and Mathematics Council (see Useful addresses). The Connexions service has information about Modern

Apprenticeships and job opportunities. Jobs are also advertised in the local press.

Photography

The popular image of a photographer is of someone shooting top models at a fashion launch or dashing after a speeding car to make a fortune with a shot of a world celebrity. In fact a photographer is more likely to make a living taking wedding photographs or family portraits.

The major development in recent years has been computerised digital imaging, enabling photographers to manipulate images and form new ones. It's not certain how far digital imaging will affect the demand for traditional photos using film, but it is certainly extending the range of services available.

Job opportunities

The three main areas of employment are:

1   Photo-processing – in three types of laboratory:

  ★ wholesale photo-finishing labs – offering a developing and printing service to the amateur photographer;
  ★ minilabs – offering high-speed services to the amateur photographer;
  ★ professional labs – providing a wide range of high quality, specialist services to professional photographers.

  All these labs are likely to offer digital services in some form or other.

2   Photography – most photographers specialise in a particular type of photography, such as:

  ★ general practice and social photography;
  ★ advertising, fashion and editorial photography;

- ★ press photography;
- ★ medical photography – making records used in hospitals, possibly using special techniques such as microphotography (photographs of very small objects);
- ★ industrial photography – recording industrial processes;
- ★ scientific photography – recording experiments and research material;
- ★ forensic photography – usually for the police force.

3 Digital imaging

- ★ This involves using computer techniques rather than chemical processes to produce a photograph. Scanning the image to digital form allows for manipulation such as removing unwanted items such as dustbins or posts, changing the background or enhancing the appearance of figures.

Skills and qualities needed

Photographers working with people need good communication skills to put subjects at their ease. They also need to have strong artistic skills and a determination to succeed. Many photographers are self-employed and run their own business affairs, which demands organisation and self-discipline.

Prospects

The largest number of jobs are in photo-processing rather than photography, but these jobs are interesting and worthwhile in themselves.

Salary

Top photographers earn high salaries but are the exception rather than the rule. An assistant to a photographer earns around £190 a week. Established photographers can expect to earn £600-plus.

Ways into work

Foundation and Advanced Modern Apprenticeships (see Introduction) leading to NVQs/SVQs at Levels 2 and 3 are available in:

★ photography
★ processing
★ controlling minilab operations
★ digital imaging.

The most usual way into a career as a photographer is by starting as a photographer's assistant, helping with shoots, checking locations, loading film, transporting equipment, making coffee and cleaning the studio. It isn't necessary to have a formal qualification for such a post and some photographers look for a keen interest in photography rather than qualifications. Assistants may be given time off for day release study. The most usual course taken is the City and Guilds 7474 Photography Competencies.

Finding a job

For information about Modern Apprenticeships contact the local Learning and Skills Council. The local Connexions service will have information about Modern Apprenticeships and job opportunities.

Useful addresses

Information technology

British Computer Society
1 Sandford Street
Swindon SN1 1HJ
Tel: 01793 417417
Website: www.bcs.org.uk

E-skills UK
1 Castle Lane
London SW1E 6DR
Website: www.e-skills.com

Institute of IT Training
Institute House
Sir William Lyons Road
University of Warwick Science Park
Coventry CV4 7EZ
Tel: 02476 418128
Website: www.iitt.org.uk

Science

Institute of Science Technology
Stowe House
Netherstowe
Lichfield
Staffs WS13 6TJ
Tel: 01543 266823
Website: www.istonline.org.uk

Science, Technology and Mathematics Council
22 Old Queen Street
London SW1H 9HP
Website: www.stmc.org.uk

Photography

British Institute of Professional Photography
Fox Talbot House
2 Amwell End
Ware
Herts SG12 9HN
Tel: 01920 464011
Website: www.bipp.com

Publications

Careers in Computing & IT, Kogan Page, £8.99.
Getting into IT and the Internet, Trotman, £9.99.
Questions and Answers Career Guides: Computing, Photography, Science. All available from Trotman, £4.99.
Working in Information Technology, Connexions, £5.50.
Working in Photography, Connexions, £5.00
Working in Science, Connexions, £6.00.

Work in retail, marketing or advertising

10

Retail

Retail operations vary from small, family owned shops and market stalls to national organisations such as Debenhams and global operations such as Tesco and The Body Shop. It isn't necessary to have a shop to run a retail operation. Mail order companies or e-retail companies offer a home delivery service to customers who buy products from catalogues or through the Internet.

Job opportunities

These include the following:

★ retail assistant
★ department or store manager
★ display/visual merchandiser.

Skills and qualities needed

Retail assistants have to know the products they are selling so they can talk to customers about them. Patience, a friendly manner and a sense of humour are essential.

Managers need all these qualities too. They also need to motivate staff, make quick decisions and take control when necessary. Good organisational skills and business awareness are important.

Visual merchandisers arrange in-store and window displays to attract customers into the store to stimulate buying. To do this job they need artistic flair and a good sense of colour and to be prepared to work as part of a team. They will often meet customers so politeness and a friendly manner are also important.

Salary

Sales assistants usually earn around £164 a week and managers between £250 and £480. Senior managers in large stores can earn more than £961 a week. Visual merchandisers earn around £288 a week. Most stores provide staff with benefits such as discounts.

Prospects

Larger stores may offer retail assistants the opportunity of promotion to senior sales posts and to supervisory or management positions. Some companies run their own management training programmes and many store managers began their careers as assistants. In turn retail managers can progress to area or regional management or head office positions.

There are good work opportunities for visual merchandisers with recognised qualifications – in shops, airports, cruise liners, museums, libraries, pubs and with local authorities.

Ways into work

Information on the industry can be found on Skillsmart's website www.skillsmart.com, which also provides online advice and guidance.

Skillsmart also produces a half-yearly publication, *Retail Therapy*, which is available free to all young people. The Institute of Grocery Distribution has information on careers in the food industry on www.careerschoices.org.uk.

Retail assistant

There are no formal qualifications needed to work as a retail assistant, although most companies may ask for GCSEs at grades A–C, Scottish Standard grades 1–3, while others will require at least some A-levels. Foundation and Advanced Modern Apprenticeships are available for young people wanting a career in retail, leading to an NVQ/SVQ Levels 2 or 3. NVQs/SVQs are available from Level 1 to 4 in Retail Operations.

Department or store manager

Entry to company management training programmes is open to those applicants who are over 18. Academic requirements are usually a minimum of A-levels/Higher grades or an equivalent qualification. Training is around 18 months to 2 years. It often includes periods of training in a college or company training centre.

Colleges and the awarding bodies such as the London Chamber of Commerce and Industry Examination Board (LLCIEB) run courses leading to qualifications in retail customer service, business studies and marketing, including Vocational A-levels (formerly Advanced GNVQs).

Visual merchandiser

It is possible to move into visual merchandising after working as a retail assistant and helping with displays. No academic qualifications are required. NVQs/SVQs are available in Interior or Exhibition Design at Levels 2–4.

However many people do start with a full-time college course, leading to British Display Society (BDS) qualifications:

★ **General Certificate in Display** – a one-year full-time course;
★ **Technician Certificate** – a one year part-time intensive study course.

Neither course requires any particular entry qualifications. Several colleges offer full-time courses such as the BTEC National Diploma in Design. In Scotland the GSVQ Level 3 in Design has display and exhibition options.

Finding a job

It is always best to first approach the company that you wish to work for; most advertise their vacancies in the stores or on their websites and from time to time in local newspapers. Alternatively speak to your local Connexions service or visit your local college which will be able to provide you with more information. Information on Modern Apprenticeships is available from the Learning and Skills Council.

You can also contact the Retail Careerline freephone on 0800 093 5001.

Case Study

Paula Pettitt
Retail Manager

During her A-level course, Paula was undecided what to do next.

'I live in a rural area so going to university would have meant moving away. I didn't feel strongly enough about taking a degree to do that. When I was 15 years old I had a work experience placement at The Body Shop in Bury St Edmunds and afterwards was offered a Saturday job there. After finishing school I decided to take a year out and worked at The Body Shop full time while I decided what to do. As the months passed and I was enjoying the work the thought of moving on became more distant, especially when I was offered the post of assistant manager.

'I was made manager of the shop when I was 21 which means I'm in charge of recruiting and training staff, ordering and merchandising stock. It's up to me to make sure the shop looks inviting and staff are welcoming. It's also my job to see that all the trading figures add up andare sent to The Body Shop head office regularly.

'The Bury St Edmunds shop is a franchise operation, which means that we have quite a lot of control over how we operate. Since I've been there I've been on a lot of training courses, learning about new products and also how to manage people and run the shop.

'The worst part of the retail industry is working weekends, but personally I wouldn't want to work anywhere else. The products we sell are very good and I love the way stock changes so quickly, with new products coming in to keep up with fashion trends.'

Marketing

The job of a marketing agency or department is to identify customer needs, research opportunities in the market, advise on product development and communicate products to customers in order to increase sales.

For example, before a food company decides to develop a new range of cereal bars, its marketing department carries out research into existing customer trends, investigating gaps in the market and considering possible ways to promote and launch the new product. Depending on the findings of this research, the company might launch a new range and support it with a marketing campaign, which could include activities such as advertising, competitions and in-store promotions.

Job opportunities

Many large companies have their own marketing department, but others bring in the services of a specialist agency. Degree courses in marketing can lead to a position as a graduate trainee.

Skills and qualities needed

Working in marketing needs strong communication skills, including listening very carefully to what a client is saying. The work can involve dealing with several different companies at the same time, so it is necessary to be well organised. Imagination and enthusiasm are important, and so is the ability to work as part of a team.

Salary

A marketing trainee could expect to earn around £200 a week, while a marketing manager can earn £865 a week or more.

Ways into work

Most entrants are over 18 and usually hold a formal marketing qualification.

The Chartered Institute of Marketing (CIM) awards qualifications at different levels:

★ **Introductory Certificate in Marketing** covers basic skills and is open to anyone over 17. Previous experience and academic qualifications are not necessary.

★ **Certificate in Marketing** can be taken by anyone over 18 who has the Introductory Certificate, five GCSEs or equivalent qualification. Those over 19 years with minimum of one year full-time experience in marketing or an NVQ/SVQ Level 2 in any subject are also eligible.

★ **Advanced Certificate in Marketing** is open to candidates with the Certificate in Marketing/CIM Certificate in Marketing Management Practice, BTEC Higher National Certificate/Diploma in any subject, NVQ/SVQ Level 3 in Marketing, NVQ/SVQ Level 4 in any other subject, other qualifications approved by CIM, three years' work experience in marketing, or a degree.

Study for these qualifications can be full or part time, intensive, online or by distance learning. Further information is available from CIM – see under Useful addresses.

The Communication, Advertising and Marketing Education Foundation (CAM) offers Advanced Certificates in six subjects. Minimum entry requirements are five GCSEs at grades A–C, Scottish Standard grades 1–3, including Maths and English. Individuals completing all six Advanced Certificates are awarded an Advanced Diploma in Communication Studies and can go on to take higher-level CAM qualifications. Study methods are flexible including evening classes and distance learning. To find out more contact CAM direct – see under Useful addresses.

Finding a job

CAM produces a booklet entitled *Getting A Job in Marketing*. Further information about a career in marketing is available from local Connexions offices. Vacancies for jobs with training are likely to be advertised in the local press and in specialist publications such as *Campaign*, *Marketing* and *Marketing Week*.

Case Study

Julian Thompson
Business Development Manager with Guardian Direct Marketing

Aged 27, Julian left school with A-levels in Sociology, Economics and History intending to go to university. Julian explains:

'I liked the idea of going to university, but couldn't decide what to study, so I took a year out, worked for a removal company and travelled in the States. On my return I worked for a landscape gardener and a seed company. Then, still

117

filling in time, I did some selling – both door to door and telesales. The experience was great, but I wasn't earning enough to survive and needed a steady job.

'I applied for a job in the warehouse at Guardian, but didn't get it! A few days later I had a call. Someone had read my CV, noticed my sales experience and wondered if I'd be interested in a job as a sales executive. The pay was low, but the job had possibilities so I took it. In six years the job has grown and so have I. We work for some impressive clients – football clubs, television companies, national newspapers, multinational companies – our range of services is growing all the time.

'We organise print buying, mail out material and run a data capture service, analysing reader response to competitions or special offers. We now have our own creative department.

'I've been sent on a number of training courses and gained a BTEC Certificate in Business at evening class.

'What I like about my job is that I feel valued and that my opinion is heard. What a blessing I didn't get the warehouse job – heaven knows where I'd be!'

Advertising

Advertisements on TV, radio, posters, the Internet, and in the press, inform people about the existence of a product or a service and try to influence their opinion of it. In the case of an ice cream or a holiday the aim of the advertisement is to persuade people to buy it, but that is not always the case. Charities advertise in the hope of donations and political parties advertise in order to attract votes. The government is the largest advertiser in the country and spends millions of pounds on recruitment and information campaigns.

Job opportunities

Most advertisers put their advertising campaigns into the hands of a specialist agency, which does the entire job, from

118

designing the advertisements to producing them and placing them with the media, for example in newspapers and on television.

Creative jobs
★ Copywriter – writing the words for the advertisements.
★ Art director – designing the advertisements.

Production jobs
★ Traffic – in charge of ensuring that departments work together and the campaign keeps to schedule.
★ Epro (electronic production) – working on sophisticated computer programs to produce the final material.

Account jobs
★ Account planning – deciding the strategies needed for a successful campaign, carrying out research into existing customers and looking at ways to attract new ones. Account planners are involved throughout a campaign, making sure original aims are not lost and clients' needs are met.
★ Media buying – deciding where and when an advertisement is to be placed and buying television, newspaper or display space. Prices can vary immensely and media executives have to negotiate the best deal possible.
★ Account executive – bringing in work, meeting potential clients, giving presentations. Once a contract has been won account executives keep in regular contact with clients, informing them of progress and reporting back to colleagues.

Skills and qualities needed

Energy, enthusiasm and the ability to work as part of a team are vital, so is tact and a sense of humour. Good communication skills are necessary, along with an organised attitude to work.

Salary

Pay levels vary greatly according to the size of the company and its geographical position. Trainees may start on salaries of around £230 a week. Top salaries for successful advertising personnel can reach six figures.

Ways into work

There are no set entry requirements. Colleges offer a range of full-time and part-time courses in advertising, business, media and communications, which will prepare students for a career in advertising but do not guarantee a job.

On-the-job training is available in the form of NVQs/SVQs at Levels 3 and 4 in Advertising and Public Relations.

The Communication, Advertising and Marketing Education Foundation (CAM) runs six Advanced Certificate courses (see section on Marketing) in which it is possible to specialise in advertising. The Institute of Practitioners in Advertising offers training courses for staff in some agencies.

Finding a job

The Advertising Association has a publication on its website entitled *Getting into Advertising* plus a recommended reading list. The Institute of Practitioners in Advertising also has information about finding a job on its website.

Further information about a career in marketing is available from local Connexions offices. Vacancies for jobs with training are likely to be advertised in the local press and in specialist publications such as *Adline, Campaign, Marketing* and *Marketing Week*.

Useful addresses

Retail

British Display Society
146 Welling Way
Welling
Kent DA16 2RS
Tel: 020 8856 2030

Skillsmart Retail Ltd
Retail Sector Skills Council
21 Dartmouth Street
London SW1H 9BP
Tel: 020 7854 8991
Website: www.skillsmart.com

Marketing

Chartered Institute of Marketing (CIM)
Education Department
Moor Hall
Cookham
Maidenhead
Berks SL6 9QH
Tel: 01628 427120
Website: www.cim.co.uk

Communication, Advertising and Marketing Education
Foundation (CAM)
Moor Hall
Cookham
Maidenhead
Berks SL6 9QH
Tel: 01628 427180
Website: www.camfoundation.com

Advertising

The Advertising Association
Abford House
15 Wilton Road
London SW1V 1NJ
Tel: 020 7828 2771
Website: www.adassoc.org.uk (look under Information Centre)

Communication, Advertising and Marketing Education Foundation (CAM)
Moor Hall
Cookham
Maidenhead
Berks SL6 9QH
Tel: 01628 427180
Webiste: www.camfoundation.com

The Institute of Practitioners in Advertising
44 Belgrave Square
London SW1X 8QS
Tel: 020 7235 7020
Website: www.ipa.co.uk

Publications

Careers in Retailing, Kogan Page, £8.99.
Getting into Retailing, Trotman, £9.99.
Media Careers in Advertising, Purple House, £8.99.
Questions and Answers Career Guides: Advertising, Marketing, Retail Industry. All available from Trotman, £4.99.
Working in Marketing and Sales, Connexions, £6.00.
Working in Retailing, Connexions, £5.00.

Work in transport

11

An efficient transport system, whether by land, sea or air, is essential to the success of many businesses. However efficient a production process may be, a company must be able to deliver goods promptly if it is to prosper.

As international trade grows and products, including perishable items such as food and flowers, are moved from country to country, so the need for efficient transport systems grows in importance.

Air

The aviation industry employs hundreds of thousands of people across the UK and transports passengers and freight to all parts of the world.

Job opportunities

★ airline pilots – flying aircraft on long and short haul flights;
★ air cabin crew – looking after passengers;
★ air maintenance engineers – inspecting, servicing and repairing aircraft;
★ air traffic controllers (ATCO) – ensuring the 5000 aircraft that fly over UK airspace daily take off, travel and land safely.

Almost all jobs in the industry involve shift and weekend work.

Skills and qualities needed

Airline pilots
Pilots need to be practical, confident and level headed, able to remain calm under pressure. Pilots need strong powers of

concentration and good communication skills, and they need to understand complicated technical material and be able to make mathematical calculations. Normal colour vision, good eyesight and good hearing are essential.

Air cabin crew

The crew work with many different people, some of whom are nervous of flying, so they have to be reassuring and polite in all circumstances. They need to be able to stay calm in emergencies and be physically fit. Good communication skills are important and so is working as part of a team.

Aircraft maintenance engineers

These engineers must work accurately and efficiently at all times even when under pressure to finish a job quickly. They need to have strong practical skills and be able to understand and follow manuals and drawings. Teamwork is important.

Air traffic controllers

A calm head is vital, and so is the ability to concentrate completely on the job. Controllers work as part of a team but also have to make decisions for themselves. They need strong technical skills to understand complicated radar and computer systems and good communication skills in order to give clearly understood directions. Normal colour vision, good eyesight and hearing are essential.

Salaries

Rates of pay vary with different airlines and the type of aircraft being flown. A captain who is in overall charge of the plane is likely to earn between £735 and £1250 a week. A first officer or co-pilot earns between £403 and £673 a week.

Air cabin crew's basic starting salary is likely to be between £157 and £163 a week. Added to these figures are flight allowances and commission for in-flight sales. British Airways cabin crew earn between £240 and £269 a week in their first year. All salaries increase with experience.

Air maintenance engineers without licences earn between £288 and £346 a week. The basic salary for licensed technicians is between £326 and £442 a week. These figures can be increased by shift allowances.

Qualified air traffic controllers start on a salary of between £600 and £638 a week. This figure can go up to £1076 a week for experienced air traffic controllers in responsible positions.

Prospects

Promotion for airline pilots is from first officer to captain and depends on having the right qualities and experience (flying hours and ratings) and on vacancies arising. It usually takes between seven and ten years to reach the position of captain.

There are opportunities for cabin crew to become cabin service managers, senior cabin attendants or pursers, or to transfer to ground administration duties.

Aircraft maintenance engineers can become senior engineers and move into supervisory posts or management positions.

Air traffic controllers progress through three grades – ATCO 3, ATCO 2 and ATCO 1. ATCO 1 is a management grade.

Ways into work

Airline pilot

There are three types of flying licence:

★ the Private Pilot's Licence (PPL)
★ the Commercial Pilot's Licence (CPL)
★ the Airline Transport Pilot's Licence (ATPL).

An ATPL is needed to fly a commercial passenger plane. This can be gained through a private training school, at a cost of up to £60,000. Potential trainees have to pass an assessment programme and usually require a minimum of five GCSEs at grades A–C or Scottish Standard grades 1–3 including English, Maths and a science or an equivalent qualification. Some schools may require A-levels, Vocational A-levels or AS-levels.

Airlines offer full or partial sponsorship for trainee airline pilots. Academic requirements are the same as for private training schools plus two A-levels or Higher grades, preferably including Maths and Physics, or equivalent qualifications in science or engineering. Entry age is usually between 18 and 28. Most airlines require pilots to pay back part of their training costs over five years.

Pilots with 150 hours' flying experience who trained with the armed forces or other organisations can train through a modular route. This involves attendance at a training school to cover the necessary theory. It takes around 26 weeks and costs a minimum of £20,000.

Training, whether privately funded or sponsored, takes place at private training schools and normally lasts between 40 and 70 weeks. It includes theory and practice and trainees finish with a Commercial Pilot's Licence and a 'frozen' ATPL. This enables them to work as a first officer or co-pilot under the command of a captain. After they have gained 1500 hours' flying experience, including specified night, cross-country and instrument flying, hold an Instrument Rating and multi-crew rating with a minimum of 500 hours as a pilot on multi-pilot aeroplanes under Instrument Flight Rules (IFR) they are awarded the ATPL.

Air cabin crew

Entry requirements vary. Some airlines want applicants to be educated to GCSE standard and others require four or five

GCSEs at grades A–C/Scottish Standard grades 1–3 including Maths and English, or equivalent qualifications. The minimum age is usually 19–21 and applicants must be of an acceptable weight in proportion to their height.

Knowledge of a second language is helpful, and essential for work with British Airways. Many airlines prefer their cabin crew to have experience of work in areas such as catering, retail or nursing. First aid qualifications are useful and so is the ability to swim, and a life-saving certificate.

Airlines have their own training schools and training takes around four to six weeks and includes customs and immigration, passenger care, first aid, food and drink service and sales training. Some colleges offer courses leading to the Air Cabin Crew Vocational Qualification. Short courses that last for one or two days and do not offer this qualification should be avoided.

Air maintenance engineer
Foundation and Advanced Modern Apprenticeships (see Introduction) are offered by some major airlines and independent aircraft maintenance organisations, which set their own entry requirements. Many ask for GCSEs at grades A–C/Scottish Standard grades 1–3 including English, Maths, Physics or Combined Sciences, or an equivalent qualification.

Full-time college courses, which can lead to a career as an air maintenance engineer, are:

★ **City and Guilds 2590 Aeronautical Engineering Competencies course**. Some colleges ask simply for science and maths ability, others for specific GCSE/Scottish Standard grades. This is a two year, full-time course and provides the knowledge required to gain an NVQ/SVQ Level 3.
★ **SQA National Certificate in Aeronautical Engineering**, which requires GCSE/Scottish Standard

passes at A–C or 1–3 in English, Maths and a science/technology subject. This is offered at Perth College and lasts one year.

★ **BTEC National Diploma in Engineering (Aerospace Engineering, Maintenance Engineering or Aerospace Studies)**. This usually requires four GCSEs at grades A–C/Scottish Standard passes 1–3 in English, Maths and a science that includes physics, or an equivalent qualification. It is offered at several colleges and is open to students and employees sponsored by companies.

Training is linked to the licensing system, which enables engineers to check and certify their own work and that of other people. The common European aircraft maintenance licence is known as Joint Aviation Requirement (JAR) 66. To gain JAR 66 engineers must complete a basic training course or an exam and gain relevant work experience. Only full-time Civil Aviation Authority (CAA) courses lead to the full JAR 66 licence.

Air traffic controller

Most ATCOs are employed by National Air Traffic Services Ltd (NATS). The majority work at area control centres, controlling planes in the sky, but others work at airports and deal with planes taking off and landing.

Applicants need to be between 18 and 27 with GCSE passes at A–C/Scottish Standard passes at 1–3, plus A-level or Higher grades or an equivalent qualification. They have to pass two selection stages.

NATS initial training lasts 74 weeks at the College of Air Traffic Control near Bournemouth and varies according to the type of work individuals will be doing and whether they will be working at area control centres or at airports. After the initial training period students are posted to a unit to train as an ATCO, where they receive practical training and work towards a Certificate of Competency.

Finding a job

For information about Modern Apprenticeships contact the local Learning and Skills Council. The Connexions service has information about job training and opportunities.

Competition for sponsored pilot-training places is very tough. Cabair College of Air Training (see under Useful addresses) publishes a list of airlines that sponsor students.

The number of air cabin crew is increasing. Some are employed by airlines that fly around the world, while others operate on a Europe-wide basis. Anyone interested in air cabin crew work should write to airlines direct.

Larger companies tend to run training programmes while smaller companies recruit trained aircraft maintenance engineers. Competition for places is severe, but there is a great demand for trained engineers.

At present National Air Traffic Services is recruiting around 116 student ATCOs a year (see Useful addresses).

Land

Rail

Until 1994 the rail industry was a single, government-owned company. Today there are 25 operating companies responsible for running passenger train services across the country. There are also infrastructure companies that manage and maintain the track and operations, and freight-operating companies which train manufacturers, maintainers and rail support operations.

Job opportunities

Rail opportunities include:

- ★ train driver
- ★ shunter
- ★ signaller
- ★ planning and scheduling
- ★ sales staff/revenue protection
- ★ ticketing
- ★ catering staff
- ★ station staff
- ★ control room operator

- ★ track engineer
- ★ civil engineer
- ★ signal and telecoms engineer
- ★ electrification engineer
- ★ on-track plant operator
- ★ rolling stock engineer
- ★ finance
- ★ information technology
- ★ human resources.

Skills and qualities needed

Anyone working in the rail industry needs a strong awareness of safety issues. Concentration at all times is vital, even when the work is routine. Staff dealing with the public have to be patient and courteous and need good communication skills.

Salary

Salaries vary widely, for example trained ticketing staff can earn from £173 to £423 a week. Drivers earn between £307 and £560 a week.

Ways into work

Foundation and Advanced Modern Apprenticeships (see Introduction), leading to NVQs/SVQs at Level 2 or 3, are available in Rail Engineering and in Rail Operations.

Although 18 is the minimum age to train as a train driver on London Underground, many companies operating on the main network will not consider applicants under 21. Safety is a vital issue, strict regulations apply and drivers have to undergo regular assessments throughout their career. Some train operating companies carry out driver training themselves, while others put it in the hands of specialist training providers. Qualifications for drivers include

NVQ/SVQ Level 2 in Rail Transport Operations (Driving) and City and Guilds 7487.

Finding a job

For information about Modern Apprenticeships contact your local Learning and Skills Council or Connexions Service. Further information about careers in the rail industry is available on www.careersinrail.org or from the Centre for Rail Skills (see Useful addresses).

Case Study

Colette Mulkeirins

Colette works for Carillion, a railway maintenance company. She is part of a maintenance team responsible for checking signals, tracks, points and other equipment. Aged 22, she has worked for Carillion for five years.

After taking GCSEs Colette followed the advice gained from a careers interview and thought about civil engineering as a career. She joined a training scheme run by the Construction Industry Training Board but was unable to find a sponsor for her course.

In Colette's words,

'At the time I was looking for sponsorship I was offered a place on a pilot course, run by the Railway Training Scheme, and decided to take it. I joined Carillion and within six months was offered a Modern Apprenticeship by the company. Since completing my apprenticeship and gaining an NVQ at Levels 2 and 3 in Railway Maintenance I have done courses in signalling, powered plant and safety.

'My day usually runs from 7.00 am to 4.00 pm. As soon as I arrive I pick up a work sheet and join my team. There are usually five of us and we're briefed on the work we're to do before going out. Once we all know what we're doing and how to carry out the work safely, we set off with our tools and equipment.

'I never wake up and feel miserable about having to go to work, because I like it so much. Railways are always likely to be there, so I have job security. Working outside means you get used to the weather, and while I may be out in the rain when other people are inside, I'm out in the sun when they're stuck in an office.'

Road

Not only do many people rely on local and national bus services for travel, over 85 per cent of goods are carried across the country by road haulage companies, varying in size from small companies with a single vehicle to organisations with a thousand-vehicle fleet.

The type of driving licence required depends upon the sort of vehicle to be driven:

★ Large Goods Vehicles (LGV) licence is required to drive vehicles above 3.5 tonnes.
★ Category C1 licence is required to drive a vehicle between 3.5 and 7.5 tonnes.
★ Category C licence is for vehicles over 7.5 tonnes.
★ Category C+E licence for articulated vehicles.
★ Passenger Carrying Vehicle (PCV) licence is required to drive a bus with more than nine passenger seats.

Job opportunities

These include delivery drivers and bus drivers.

Skills and qualities needed

Work involves long periods on the road, so drivers need to enjoy driving, have good powers of concentration and be reasonably fit and healthy with good eyesight. They need good practical driving skills and the patience to deal with other drivers on the road. Bus drivers dealing with members of the public need to be tactful and to get on well with all types of people.

Salary

Drivers can earn between £192 and £330 a week depending on the company and the type of vehicle driven. There may also be the possibility of overtime work.

Prospects

There is no set promotion ladder for drivers, but there are opportunities to move into supervisory or management posts.

Ways into work

No formal academic qualifications are needed to train as a driver. Some companies train their own drivers and put them through the appropriate test. It is also possible to train privately at a specialist driving school to gain both LGV and PCV licences.

Foundation and Advanced Modern Apprenticeships are available in two frameworks: Road Haulage and Distribution, and Driving Goods Vehicles.

NVQs/SVQs are available at Levels 1–5.

The Road Haulage and Distribution Training Council, which is the national training organisation for the industry, runs a Young LGV Driver Scheme that enables trainees under 20 to follow a fast-track programme to a Category C licence at 18 years old and gain an NVQ/SVQ Level 2.

Finding a job

For information about Modern Apprenticeships contact the local Learning and Skills Council. The Connexions service has information about Modern Apprenticeships. Further information about the Young LGV Driver scheme is available from the Road Haulage and Distribution Training Council (see Useful addresses).

Sea

The Merchant Navy

Britain has a long maritime tradition and today UK waters are some of the busiest in the world, with over 90 per cent of trade arriving or leaving by sea. The Merchant Navy offers great opportunities for capable and enthusiastic young people to manage and operate modern, technically sophisticated ships.

Job opportunities

The British Merchant Fleet (Merchant Navy) consists of a large number of ships operated by individual shipping companies. It operates worldwide and includes:

★ the world's largest and most modern ferry sector;
★ some of the most prestigious cruise companies in the world;
★ containerships carrying a variety of cargo;
★ high quality oil, gas and chemical tankers of all sizes;
★ modern bulk carriers carrying ores, grain and coal;
★ specialised vessels, including support for the offshore exploration industry.

In charge of the entire ship is the master or captain. The ship's engineering and technical systems are in the charge of the chief engineer. Deck officers are responsible for controlling navigation, communications, cargo handling and ship stability. Working for them are deck ratings who have a lower level of responsibility. Engineer officers are responsible for all technical services on board and engineer ratings support them by carrying out routine maintenance and repairs.

There are some dual officer roles that cover both deck and engineering departments.

Catering and hospitality support services are required on cruise ships and passenger ferries, which are run on the lines of a large hotel. Specific roles vary between shipping companies, and generally prior qualifications and experience in the catering, hotel or hospitality industry are necessary. There are jobs for pursers/receptionists, restaurant and bar staff, housekeepers, cruise directors, entertainers, hairdressers, beauticians, photographers, child care and retail staff.

Skills and qualities needed

On board ship work is divided into shifts or watches, which are usually four hours on and eight hours off. Leave time is generous, but the job means unsocial hours and some long periods at sea depending on the type of ship and its trading pattern. Merchant seamen need to take responsibility when necessary and respond quickly to any emergencies. A sense of humour and tolerance are required to live in close contact with others. Good health and eyesight are essential.

Salaries

Pay depends on rank and the shipping company.

A rating earns between £16,000 and £21,000 a year, a junior officer earns between £17,000 and £21,000, a senior officer earns between £21,000 and £45,000. Officer cadets have tuition and course fees paid, plus a salary or training allowance of around £4500 to £7000.

Prospects

There are four main entry routes: Marine Traineeship, Marine Apprenticeship, Officer Cadet Training and Graduate Entry. Each provides promotion opportunities through to the ranks of master/captain or chief engineer.

Ways into work

Entry is at 16, 18 or 21 and above. All the training programmes have alternating periods at college and at sea. Trainees are sponsored by their training company.

★ **Marine Traineeship Deck and Engineering** – requires at least three GCSEs or Scottish Standard grades, a foundation GNVQ/GSVQ or equivalent qualification.

★ **Marine Apprenticeship Deck and Engineering** – requires at least four GCSEs or Scottish Standard grades in English, Maths, Physics or a combined science, Intermediate GNVQ or equivalent qualification.

★ **Officer Cadet Training Deck and Engineering** – requires at least four GCSEs (A–C)/Scottish Standard grades (1–3) in English, Maths, Physics or a combined science, or with A-levels or Scottish Highers or an Intermediate GNVQ/GSVQ or equivalent.

Finding a job

The Connexions service gives advice on careers in the Merchant Navy. The first step is to gain sponsorship from a shipping company or training organisation. A full list of such companies is available from the Merchant Navy Training Board (details in Useful addresses) and on the Merchant Navy website: www.mntb.org.uk.

Useful addresses

Air

Association of Licensed Aircraft Engineers
Bourn House
8 Park Street
Bagshot
Surrey GU19 5AQ
Tel: 01276 474888
Website: www.lae.mcmail.com

British Airline Pilots Association
81 New Road
Harlington
Hayes
Middlesex UB3 5BG
Tel: 020 8476 4000
Website: www.balpa.org.uk

Cabair College of Air Training
Elstree Aerodrome
Borehamwood
Herts WD6 3AW
Tel: 020 8236 2400

Civil Aviation Authority
Aviation House
Gatwick Airport South
West Sussex RH6 0YR
Tel: 01293 567171
Website: www.srg.caa.co.uk

National Air Traffic Services Ltd
London Area Control Centre
Sopwith Way
Swanwick
Southampton SO31 7AY
Tel: 01895 445566
Website: www.nats.co.uk

Royal Aeronautical Society
4 Hamilton Place
London W1J 7BQ
Tel: 020 7499 3515
Website: www.aerosociety.com

Rail

Centre for Rail Skills
PO Box 39685
London W2 IXR
Tel: 0845 345 2700
Website: www.ritc.org.uk

Road

Road Haulage and Distribution Training Council
14 Warren Yard
Warren Farm Office Village
Stratford Road
Milton Keynes MK12 5NW
Tel: 01908 313360
Website: www.rhdtc.co.uk

Sea

The Merchant Navy Training Board
12 Carthusian Street
London EC1M 6EZ
Tel: 020 7417 2800
Website: www.mntb.org.uk

Work in the uniformed services **12**

Ambulance service
British Army
Fire service
Police force
Royal Air Force
Royal Navy.

This chapter covers a wide range of careers, from the armed forces – Army, Navy and RAF – to the work of the police, fire and ambulance services.

While each of the uniformed services has a proud and long historical tradition, today's operations are based in the 21st century – using the latest technology and offering equal opportunities to young men and women from all backgrounds and ethnic groups.

Ambulance service

The majority of calls to the ambulance service are not 999 emergencies but pre-planned transfers of patients between hospitals, to outpatient appointments or home following in-patient treatment. The service is organised on a regional basis and recruitment and training vary from area to area.

Job opportunities

★ ambulance care assistant – driving and escorting routine non-emergency patients;
★ ambulance technician – working with paramedics, answering urgent calls, travelling in ambulances, air ambulances or on motorcycles and administering

pre-hospital treatment using equipment such as ventilators to ease breathing difficulties;

★ ambulance paramedic – doing similar work to a technician but also being trained to administer certain drugs and treatments without a doctor's permission.

Skills and qualities needed

Ambulance personnel need to be warm and positive, able to reassure injured and frightened people. They must be calm, be able to work as part of a team, have strong powers of concentration and good communication skills. Physical and emotional strength is important because the work can be distressing.

Salary

A qualified ambulance care assistant earns around £250 a week. An ambulance technician earns around £346 a week while a paramedic earns around £400 a week.

Prospects

Care assistants can become technicians and then paramedics. Senior managers are usually promoted from the ranks. Most ambulance personnel work in the National Health Service, but there are some openings with private services.

Ways into work

Care assistant

You must be over 18 with a clean driving licence. Some services require a good standard of education while others ask for four GCSEs at grades A–C/Scottish Standard grades 1–3 in English and Maths. Scotland also requires a science subject. Training covers driving skills and emergency accident management and is followed by a probationary period at a station.

Technician

You need to be over 21 with a clean driving licence. Some services ask for a good standard of education while others are more specific. Scotland requires two A-levels/Highers. There is a national training programme for technicians, which includes emergency care, physiology and anatomy and intensive driving techniques. After training technicians work under supervision for a year.

Paramedic

Paramedics are chosen for training from technicians after a tough selection process. The training is demanding and includes time spent in a hospital operating theatre. Paramedics have to requalify every three years.

Finding a job

The Connexions service gives advice on careers in the ambulance service. Information is also available from ambulance service headquarters, listed in the local phone directory.

Case Study

Andrew Carr
Paramedic

Andrew is a paramedic team leader. As well as responding to urgent and emergency calls he is responsible for the administration of the ambulance station. This includes drawing up work rotas, recording absences and ordering equipment.

He is trained to give treatments including intubating patients, putting a plastic tube into the windpipe to clear airways, and inserting a cannula or tube into a vein through which drugs can be given. Drugs are given by paramedics for life-threatening situations such as cardiac arrest, fitting and diabetic comas.

What can I do with... no degree?

Andrew took A-levels in Geography, Economics and Politics and went on to university.

In his words,

'It was a mistake. I was not very interested in my course. At the end of two years I decided to leave. I spent several years working in tourism in Portugal, before coming back to the UK and working with people with learning difficulties. I like caring for people, but I also like excitement, and that was what led me to apply to become a paramedic.

'There are several different pathways for paramedics, which vary slightly from area to area. I worked as a student ambulance technician for a year, then spent a year as a qualified technician before applying to become a paramedic.

'The work falls into two areas: urgent and emergency. Urgent calls are from doctors requesting that patients be taken to hospital within a set time, which could be two or four hours. Emergency calls are 999 calls that need a very quick response. We don't drive from emergency to emergency as ambulance teams do on television, but we do deal with major traumas such as traffic accidents, so paramedics need a strong stomach. They also need to be emotionally strong to cope with some depressing situations. The job can be dangerous, especially on Friday and Saturday nights when people are out drinking.

'All paramedics have to drive ambulances and pass an advanced driving course. Most importantly they also have to relate to people in any situation.

'I've been doing the job for 13 years and still find it exciting. There's the satisfaction of helping people and knowing that my high level of training means that I can make a difference between life and death.

British Army

The Army plays an important role at home and abroad, taking part in humanitarian and peacekeeping assignments and carrying out a wide range of essential duties in war.

Job opportunities

The Army is divided into two parts:

★ The Arms – made up of Combat Arms, the mainline
fighting forces, and Combat Support Arms, which operates
and fights in their support.
★ The Services – which provide technical and administrative
assistance.

Within the Arms and Services there are job opportunities in
nine areas:

★ Combat
★ Engineering
★ Logistics
★ IT/communication
★ HR/administration and finance
★ Healthcare
★ Specialist
★ Officer
★ Further education.

Skills and qualities needed

The Army prides itself on training recruits from different
backgrounds to work together as a team. Soldiers need to be
physically fit, keen to learn and eager to be part of a team.

Salary

The most junior soldier receives over £200 a week. This
increases with time served and promotion. There is a pay
review every year. For up-to-date information on rates of pay
for all ranks see the Army website www.armyjobs.co.uk.

Prospects

Promotion is based on individual merit rather than length of
service. Promotion can be rapid and soldiers with strong

leadership potential have the option to train as commissioned officers.

Ways into work

There are two main routes into the Army.

Single entry

This gives trainees aged between 16 years 9 months and 27 years direct access to over 100 different jobs, suiting a wide range of abilities. Some jobs are available to trainees up to 33 years old.

Junior entry
Army Foundation College

The college offers a one-year training programme for young people aged between 16 and 17 years 1 month who want to join the Army.

Army Development Course

This is a 17-week practical course at the Army Training Regiment at Bassingbourn for young people aged between 16 and 17 years 1 month who want to join the Army.

School Leavers Scheme

The scheme is a 32-week practical course for trainees aged 16 years 9 months.

Army training leads to NVQs/SVQs, BTECs and City and Guilds qualifications. There are also opportunities to take GCSEs, A-levels and, for those who wish, a degree.

Finding a job

Full details of opportunities are available from local Armed Forces Careers Offices, listed under 'Army' in the telephone directory. Also, have a look at the Army's careers website for teenagers at www.mycamouflage.co.uk.

Fire service

Only one in five calls to the fire service is for help with a fire. The service also assists at road, rail and air traffic accidents, chemical spillages and floods and educates the public in fire safety. There are 58 different fire brigades in England and Wales and eight in Scotland.

Job opportunities

There are three types of firefighter: wholetime, retained and volunteer. This section deals only with wholetime firefighters. There are 34,300 wholetime firefighters in the UK and there are always more applicants than vacancies.

Skills and qualities needed

Firefighters need to get on with different types of people – even those who are confused and difficult – and must be able to work under pressure as part of a team. Firefighters are practical people, physically very fit, with good eyesight, and able to cope with dangerous situations and with shift work.

Salary

A firefighter aged 18 entering the service earns £328.09 a week and a firefighter aged 24 and over earns £348.75 a week.

Prospects

All entrants begin as firefighters. There are no special entry arrangements for people with particular qualifications and promotion is on merit.

Ways into work

Entrants must be at least 18. A good standard of education is required and some brigades ask for specific GCSE passes.

There is a national fitness test and medical examination. Good vision is essential.

Initial training lasts approximately three months and includes theory and practical work. Recruits then move to a fire station where they spend a two-year probationary period. Training continues throughout a firefighter's career.

Many colleges run BTEC First and National Diploma courses in Public and Uniformed Services. These give a good idea of the type of work involved in the fire service, but they do not guarantee the offer of a place in the brigade.

Finding a job

The Connexions service gives advice on careers in the fire service. Information is also available from the recruitment departments of local fire services, listed in the local telephone directory.

Police force

Police work is not the exciting stream of bank robberies, abductions and murder hunts it appears to be on television. However for the right person it is an interesting and rewarding career. There are 43 local police forces in England and Wales and eight in Scotland. Between them they deal with 6 million 999 calls a year.

Job opportunities

Three-quarters of all police officers are constables, dealing with the public, carrying out patrols and coping with disturbances. To become a sergeant a constable must pass the Sergeants' Exam. There are then opportunities for promotion and for specialisation in areas such as CID or Special Branch.

Skills and qualities needed

Police officers need to be physically and mentally fit. They have to cope with rude and aggressive behaviour. The shift system means disturbed sleep patterns and difficulties having a social life outside the force. A sense of humour, strong observation skills, a good memory, communication skills and a desire to help people are essential.

Salary

The starting pay for a police constable is £368 a week, with pay increases at regular intervals. Five years after completion of initial training a police constable earns around £476 a week.

Prospects

Every year around 60,000 people apply to join the police and only 6,000 are accepted. New recruits spend two years as a probationary constable, working on the beat and spending time studying at one of six national police training centres. At constable level there are good opportunities to specialise and to develop an interesting career. Officers who pass the Sergeants' Exam can aim for promotion up the ranks.

Ways into work

There are no set academic requirements for becoming a police officer, although candidates must show they have a good grounding in maths and English by passing the Police Initial Recruitment Test.

Everyone goes through the same selection process. Applicants must be over 18 years and 6 months, be physically fit and have good eyesight. They also need either a clean driving licence or to be in the process of learning to drive. During selection they must show themselves to be determined, honest and enthusiastic. Rather than looking for a particular type, the police force wants interesting people who have done something with their free time, whether it is community service, self-defence or learning a foreign language.

Many colleges run BTEC First and National Diploma courses in Public and Uniformed Services. These give a good idea of the type of work involved and whether a person is suited to the police force, but they do not guarantee the offer of a job.

Finding a job

The Connexions service gives advice on careers in the police. Information is also available from the headquarters of each police force, listed in the local telephone directory.

Royal Air Force

The RAF was formed in 1918 when the Royal Flying Corps amalgamated with the Royal Naval Air Service. Today it has a force of over 50,000 men and women employed in approximately 70 disciplines.

There are three levels of entry into the RAF: commissioned officer, non-commissioned aircrew and airman/airwoman.

Job opportunities

Officer branches include pilot, weapon systems officer (navigator), air traffic controller, fighter controller, engineer, supply and administration, as well as specialists such as doctors, dentists, legal officers and chaplains.

All non-comissioned aircrew enter as weapon systems operators. Linguists are pre-streamed but all others are allocated to the specialisations of air loadmaster, acoustics or electronic warfare during their training.

Airmen/airwomen trades are many and varied (about 45 in total), from technicians to caterers, photographers to flight operations assistants and nurses to musicians.

Skills and qualities needed

All RAF personnel must be physically fit, motivated, good communicators and be able to work as part of a team. Different areas of work demand particular skills, but everyone needs to be able to operate under pressure. Officers must have leadership qualities, accept responsibility and be capable of motivating different types of people in diverse situations.

Salary

On completion of initial training, normally an officer will earn £463.75 per week. On the award of their flying brevet, non-commissioned aircrew earn £513.45 per week and airmen/airwomen earn a minimum of £287.49 per week after one year's service.

Prospects

The number of vacancies varies according to branch or trade. Promotion is awarded on individual performance against establishment vacancies. Commissions are available to all non-commissioned personnel who gain the required academic qualifications and have the right leadership qualities.

Ways into work

Basic officer entry requirements are two A-levels/Scottish Higher grades plus at least five GCSEs at grades A–C, Scottish Standard grades 1–3, including English Language and Maths. Equivalent qualifications may be acceptable. Selections are made at the Officers and Aircrew Selection Centre (OASC) at the RAF College at Cranwell in Lincolnshire.

Entry as NCO aircrew usually requires five GCSEs at grades A–C/Scottish Standard grades 1–3, including English Language and Maths. The specialisation dictates what other qualifications are needed. As for officers, selections are made at OASC.

What can I do with... no degree?

Many airmen/airwomen jobs require no formal qualifications, while others require specific subjects and grades. Every candidate has to pass aptitude tests and a medical at an Armed Forces Careers Office.

Finding a job

The Connexions service gives advice on careers in the RAF. Detailed information is available from Armed Forces Careers Offices (under Royal Air Force in the telephone directory) and from the careers website at www.rafcareers.com.

Case Study

Ben Hardy

Aged 25, Ben is a physical training instructor and a corporal in the RAF. He joined in 1996.

The RAF comprises training units and strike units. Working in a training unit, Ben's role is similar to that of a PE teacher in school. A strike unit is made up of fully trained personnel and here the role of fitness instructors is to ensure personnel are fit for operations. They set up remedial packages where necessary and organise adventurous training such as rock climbing and hill walking.

After GCSEs Ben took a two-year BTEC National Certificate Pre-Uniformed Services course at West Anglia College, King's Lynn, and was accepted for training with the Royal Marines.

He says,

'After a few months I began to feel I wanted to train for a craft that would give me a future other than being a soldier. A college friend had joined the RAF to train as a physical training instructor and, the more I spoke to him, the more drawn I was to the idea.'

Ben left the Marines and applied to the RAF, filling in the 'gap' year with casual jobs. More than five years on, he has no regrets:

'It's a fantastic life. Since joining I've gained military and civilian instructor qualifications in rock climbing, kayaking, skiing and in summer mountain leadership. The great things about the RAF are the cross-section of people you meet and the responsibility you're given from the very start. If you have a good idea people really want to hear about it.'

Royal Navy

The history of the Royal Navy dates back as far as 882, when King Alfred took part in a seaborne engagement in the Stour estuary that earned him the name 'Father of the Navy'. Today's Royal Navy is admired across the globe as a world leader.

Job opportunities

The Royal Navy is made up of four Fighting Arms:

Amphibious – this includes the Royal Marines and the amphibious task group RN vessels.
Surface Ships – maintain and operate all surface vessels.
Fleet Air Arm – maintain and operate all fixed wing and rotary aircraft.
Submarine Service – maintain and operate all submarines including the national Strategic Nuclear Deterrent.

Within these four Fighting Arms there are several Branches (or jobs) that can be grouped together as:

Warfare – tactical use of weapons systems and operation of ships and submarines.
Engineering – maintenance and operation of propulsion and generation machinery, including weapons systems.
Supply – logistical and hotel services support.
Medical – includes medical, dentistry and Queen Alexandra's Royal Naval Nursing Service (QARNNS).
Fleet Air Arm – aircraft handlers and safety equipment specialists, all of whom are trained for emergency situations.

Submarine – maintain, operate and provide logistical support to the submarine fleet.

Skills and qualities needed

Naval personnel need to be team players, able to get on with others in a confined environment. They need to be very fit, self-disciplined, yet ready to obey orders. Officers must be good communicators, quick-thinking decision makers with strong leadership skills.

Salary

Basic pay on entry for a non-technician is £213 a week.

Prospects

Entry into the Navy is as an officer or a rating. All entrants go through basic training before beginning specialist training. There is a structured promotion system. A number of naval officers began their career as ratings.

Ways into work

Minimum entry requirements for Royal Navy officers and Royal Marines officers are two A-levels/Scottish Higher grades plus at least five GCSEs at grades A–C, Scottish Standard grades 1–3, including English and Maths, or an equivalent qualification such as BTEC/SQA National Diploma or Advanced VCE/GSVQ.

Officer entrants to QARNNS need a nursing qualification and two years' experience. You can apply for a commission after two years in the service.

Royal Navy candidates have to pass a fitness test, a selection test, an interview and a medical examination. Some trades also ask for specific qualifications.

Royal Marines must have a minimum height of 1.63 metres and have to pass a three-day course comprising written tests, physical exercises and an interview.

Finding a job

The Connexions service gives advice on careers in the Royal Navy. Information, including all available job opportunities, is available from Armed Services Careers Offices, or from Officer Careers Liaison Offices for officers' jobs, listed in the local telephone directory and on the Royal Navy website, royalnavy.mod.uk.

Useful addresses

Ambulance Service Association
Friars House
157–168 Blackfriars Road
London SE1 8EU
Tel: 020 7928 9620
Website: www.asa.uk.net

Armed Services Careers Offices
(listed in local telephone directories)

The Army website:
www.mycamouflage.co.uk

Fire service website:
www.fireservice.co.uk

Royal Air Force website:
www.raf-careers.com

Royal Navy website:
www.royal-navy.mod.uk

National Police Recruitment Call Centre
Tel: 0845 6083000
Website: www.police-information.co.uk

Publications

Getting into the Armed Forces, Trotman, £9.99.
Questions and Answers Career Guide: Armed Forces, Trotman,
£4.99.
Working in the Armed Services, COIC, £5.50.